RAISING ABEL

RAISING ABEL

THE LIFE OF FAITH

RONALD RAGOTZY, MD

BALBOA.
PRESS
A DIVISION OF HAY HOUSE

ISBN: 978-1-4525-6443-2 (sc)
ISBN: 978-1-4525-6441-8 (hc)
ISBN: 978-1-4525-6442-5 (e)

Library of Congress Control Number: 2012922535

Balboa Press books may be ordered through booksellers or by contacting:
Balboa Press
A Division of Hay House
1663 Liberty Drive
Bloomington, IN 47403
www.balboapress.com
1-(877) 407-4847

Printed in the United States of America

Balboa Press rev. date: 12/03/2012

For Declan. Thanks to my mother, Brenda, and to Patty
for all their support and demonstrations of faith

Contents

Chapter 1

Introduction
My Bible

The Bible is a book that has been read more and
examined less than any book that ever existed.
—Thomas Paine (1737–1809)[1]

FAITH[2] IS THE HIGHEST CREATION of the universe, and we are its keepers. I must have been born with this idea imprinted on my brain. I cannot remember a time when I cared more about anything. Even as I prepared for my wedding day, I was more interested in talking to the priest about what faith really was and how I could express it than I was in reciting my marriage vows. At the time I was told that getting married was an act of keeping faith and that I should be satisfied with that, but I was not. I wanted to do more—much more.

1 ThinkExist.com Quotations. "Thomas Paine quotes". ThinkExist.com Quotations Online 1 Oct. 2012. 19 Nov. 2012 <http://en.thinkexist.com/quotes/thomas_paine/5.html>

2 Faith cannot be defined in words; we must use metaphors to begin to discuss what faith is or is not.

One of the things I felt I needed to do to learn more about faith was to reconcile my thinking about faith with the Bible with which I grew up. For most of my adult life, I had felt that I could not keep reading Genesis 1–11 as a literal history of the world. The stories of creation, Adam and Eve, Cain and Abel, Noah's ark, and the Tower of Babel—also known as the primeval history—had become an ineffective reflection of faith for me. Reading them literally was not helping me experience faith. Because it lost its impact on me, I put the Bible aside for many years. During that time in my life, I was a husband, a father, and even a doctor; but I was not a keeper of faith. I felt empty and did not know what to do. I may have had a thread of faith that I was trying to cling to, but I did not have the faith I wanted. I knew that if I were to return to the Bible, I would need to go deeper into the text to find the faith I was looking for—much deeper.

By deeper I mean that I knew I must use all the tools at my disposal to understand the messages in Genesis 1–11. One very powerful way to deepen my understanding of Scripture was to read the stories as metaphors for faith. This way of reading the Bible is called an anagogical[3] interpretation. To read Genesis 1–11 anagogically, all I needed to do was ask myself how the images presented in the stories related to faith.

Let me give an example with the story of Cain and Abel. Cain and Abel were brothers, but metaphorically they can also represent two different aspects of a person. Since Abel was the brother who was accepted by God,[4] it is easy to see that he is a metaphor for the faith that resides in each of us. Cain, on the other hand, is a metaphor for the self-will[5] side of us, since he did everything on his own. He certainly did not listen to what God told him to do. Cain did not even answer when God asked him why he was so angry. Instead, Cain unleashed his anger on Abel and killed him. Even when God tried to engage Cain a second time by asking him where his brother was, he replied back with a question: "Am I my brother's keeper?" Cain showed that he was more than willing to go through life not listening to anyone but

3 Anagogical refers to interpretation using spiritual metaphors (e.g., the tree of life represents faith).

4 God and LORD God are also terms that cannot be defined in words; we must use metaphors to begin to discuss what they are or are not.

5 Self-will is the same thing as the knowledge of good and evil, and in this book, it is also interchangeable with other terms, including reason, belief, judgment, and wisdom. They all represent forms of human intellectual thought as opposed to faith, which is not a form of human intellectual thought.

himself, and therefore he was the embodiment of a life based on self-will and not on faith.

Reading the Cain and Abel story with the brothers representing the two sides of each of us gives a much deeper insight into how faith relates to self-will. With this metaphor, we can see that faith and self-will are like brothers. The Bible is telling us that the role of our self-will is to be the big brother and keeper of our faith, protecting it from a sometimes-cruel world. But if our self-will rejects the job of keeper, then our faith side will surely perish.

Genesis 1–11 contains dozens of metaphors that explain and connect the individual stories so we can better understand faith. We will explore many of them in the following chapters, but we must be careful with this kind of interpretation. We can learn a lot from seeing the Genesis stories through a metaphoric lens, but we must also know the limits of the metaphors.

Inherent in the use of metaphors in understanding any text is that they must be only temporary images. The metaphors deepen our understanding of the stories but are not meant to be included in the original written text. We must not change the text permanently. If we insist that a given metaphor is the only true way to read the text, then we severely limit the Bible's potential for speaking to all people in all times. One example of a metaphor that has changed the original meaning of the text for many is found in one common interpretation of Genesis 3. Many people view the serpent in the story of the garden of Eden as the actual Devil. I think everyone can understand that the serpent can be a metaphor for the Devil or the incarnation of evil, but if we limit the metaphor, it can prevent us from understanding all the possibilities in the story. Seeing the serpent as the Devil prevents us from using the serpent as a metaphor for Eve's own self-will or even recognizing that the serpent might represent a force that may have been attempting to help Eve not to eat the fruit of the tree of the knowledge of good and evil. If we do not use metaphors as temporary images, then we destroy any chance the Bible has to help everyone experience a deeper faith. Preserving the original images in the stories allows us a multitude of other readings and metaphors, permitting a deepening and evolving understanding of faith. They are not meant to alter the original text, but it is in discovering and working with the metaphors that we grow in faith. Metaphors are the words in the language of faith.

Any metaphor that I use in this book is only meant for a deeper understanding of faith as presented in Genesis 1–11 and is not intended to be a permanent interpretation of the text. I believe that if we do not use metaphors to interpret the text, we will be missing out on the full and complex meanings contained in the greatest book ever written. What is a fine interpretation at one point in our lives can become stale as we grow. But if we continue to read, the metaphors change, and as they change, so do we. I believe that uncovering the metaphors found in Genesis 1–11 takes us on a journey of faith. This is exactly what happened to me with my reading of the Bible. For years I was not encouraged to see new metaphors in the stories of Genesis 1–11, so I put the Bible aside and was at risk for never seeing the deeper beauty of the primeval history.

It is no wonder that people resist any interpretation of the Bible other than the literal interpretation. We have not been taught to use metaphors as tools to explore deeper meanings of this text. I can even remember being warned not to try to interpret the Bible myself because it was too dangerous. However, having failed to find faith reading the Bible in the way others told me to, I just had to try and see what the stories meant to me as metaphors. It may have been a dangerous venture, but I could not accept the alternative—a life without real faith. When I read the primeval history as a metaphor for what faith was and how it related to me, the stories exploded with insights and connectivity. They were now really engaging me, but this time in the language I could understand.

The individual stories not only started to really speak to me, but I also began to see why Genesis 1–11 included the exact stories in the exact order that it did. Before I saw the metaphors, the stories of creation, Adam and Eve, Cain and Abel, Noah's ark, and the Tower of Babel seemed like unrelated, random tales. When the metaphors revealed themselves, each story became a part of a bigger picture. Like a jigsaw puzzle, each story's images were individual pieces, and when put together, they made one complete picture—a picture of faith. This linking together of stories is called concatenation. Seeing the new metaphors and discovering how the stories connected to each other became very exhilarating to me, and I wanted to read and explore more of the Bible every chance I got. I'll admit that sometimes I would intentionally avoid the Bible altogether, not daring to open the cover because if I did, two or three hours would elapse before I paused for a breather. It was that compelling. I was beginning to experience faith on a whole new level and intensity that I did not think I could fully comprehend myself, let alone share with others.

At that point, I must admit, I was also feeling a little secretive. Who would share my new enthusiasm for Genesis 1–11? Not the people who read the Bible literally; they would tell me it was too dangerous. Not the people, like me, who had given up on the Bible; they would just make fun of me. I was afraid they would say, "You're reading the Bible again; how 'original.'" Not the biblical scholars; they did not seem to be interested in keeping faith, just in discussing the origins of the text. Not the atheists. They were not interested in reading the Bible metaphorically. They could not prove a metaphor right or wrong; they could only argue against a literal interpretation. But I had to tell somebody. It was going to leak out in my conversations anyway. I couldn't stop it.

When I did tell individuals, the response was unanimous. They were all very interested and listened intently; one person even told me that she got goose bumps. These people also told me that if I ever wrote a book about Genesis, they would like to read it. I was hoping their requests were genuine and that they needed the metaphors written down to make it easier for them to digest each one, hoping they were not just trying to get me to stop talking to them. But I took their request seriously and started to write down and organize the metaphors I found. What follows is a framework of the Genesis 1–11 metaphors I have discovered so far.

The fundamental message goes something like this: Genesis 1, the creation story, is a poem about faith. I have heard many times that Genesis 1 was written more like a song, but I had never heard anyone say anything about what the song/poem was about. It was easy to see that the poem in Genesis 1 described the creation of the universe, but was the creation symbolic of something else?

Take the example of the story of Moby Dick. If we only see Moby Dick as a story about whale hunting, then we miss its message about the human struggle. Reading with a deeper meaning in mind, I believed that Genesis 1 was a poem that used the events of the physical creation of the universe to explain the characteristics of faith. It used the building of the universe as a metaphor for what faith can build in each of us. For example:

> And God said, Let the waters bring forth *abundantly* the moving creature that hath life, and fowl that may fly above the earth in the open firmament of heaven. And God created great whales, and every living creature that moveth, which the waters brought forth *abundantly*, after their kind, and every winged fowl after his kind: and God saw that it was good. (Gen. 1:20)

The word *abundant* stands out in this passage. Abundance not only describes the life in the sea, but it also applies to the inexhaustibility of faith. Faith is more abundant than all the fish in the seas and all the fowl in the heavens. With this metaphor, I not only think about what abundance means but also build on the image by imagining endless numbers of fish swimming in schools and darting around objects effortlessly. If I tried to stop the flow of fish or catch them with my hands, they would just swim around me and reassemble on the other side, as if nothing had happened. Likewise, faith flows through our lives, but we can never grab it, direct it, or contain it.

I have found many other metaphors for faith in Genesis 1; they will be discussed in detail in as I address Genesis 1. Genesis uses the six days of creation to organize these metaphors for faith. It uses things found in nature as perfect symbols of faith. We find at the end of the creation week that the ultimate metaphor for faith is rest on the seventh day. Genesis 1 may be a factual account of creation, but to me, the important message is that it tells me what faith can mean.

The next two stories—the garden of Eden and Cain and Abel—tell us why we don't readily experience faith in our lives and why we experience so much suffering. These tales tell us that we are blessed with both faith and self-will, or wisdom, to help us deal with life and that they are meant to work together. If we choose to rely solely on our own wisdom, ignoring faith, we will suffer. We see this play out when Adam and Eve are at the tree of the knowledge of good and evil. At the tree, Eve reasons:

> And when the woman saw that the tree was good for food, and that it was pleasant to the eyes, and a tree to be desired to make one wise, she took of the fruit thereof, and did eat, and gave also unto her husband with her; and he did eat. (Gen. 3:6)

Eve relied on her own wisdom and reasoning, rather than having faith in what God told her not to do. This marks the moment when Adam and Eve lost their faith. From that instant, they began to suffer. With these stories, the Bible is telling us that everyone will lose his or her faith; it is a normal occurrence in human life. But Genesis 1–11 does not leave us to forever suffer the loss of faith; it gives us the solution. The very next story about Noah gives us the answer or the prescription for how to get faith back in our lives. Noah's story gives us a practical method to reinvigorate our faith. In fact, Noah's story is the central message of Genesis 1–11, and to fully embrace the meanings of the metaphors of the ark and the flood is to fully embrace faith. Finally, the stories of Noah's nakedness and the Tower of Babel end the primeval history by telling us how to put faith into action.

The stories of Genesis 1–11 need to be *examined* repeatedly, not just read repeatedly. Each time we read them through, more metaphors will appear, allowing a deeper understanding of and connection with each story, a connection that we can apply to our lives today to experience faith. If we commit ourselves enough, we will be "Abel" to enjoy faith working in our lives, giving us great comfort, peace, and rest.

> All God wants of man is a gift of a peaceful heart.
>
> —Meister Eckhart (1260–c. 1328)[6]

---

6 ThinkExist.com Quotations. "Meister Eckhart quotes". ThinkExist.com Quotations Online 1 Oct. 2012. 19 Nov. 2012 <http://en.thinkexist.com/quotes/meister_eckhart/3.html>

Chapter 2

The Premise Defining Healthy Faith and Wisdom

Both read the Bible day and night, But thou read'st black I read white.
—William Blake (1757–1827)[7]

Genesis 1

1 In the beginning God created the heaven and the earth.
2 And the earth was without form, and void; and darkness
upon the face of the deep. And the Spirit of God moved
upon the face of the waters. 3 And God said, Let there be
light: and there was light. 4 And God saw the light, that
good: and God divided the light from the darkness. 5 And
God called the light Day, and the darkness he called Night.
And the evening and the morning were the first day. 6 And

7 ThinkExist.com Quotations. "William Blake quotes". ThinkExist.com Quotations Online 1 Oct. 2012. 19 Nov. 2012 <http://en.thinkexist.com/quotes/william_blake/7.html>

God said, Let there be a firmament in the midst of the waters, and let it divide the waters from the waters. 7 And God made the firmament, and divided the waters which under the firmament from the waters which above the firmament: and it was so. 8 And God called the firmament Heaven. And the evening and the morning were the second day. 9 And God said, Let the waters under the heaven be gathered together unto one place, and let the dry appear: and it was so.

10 And God called the dry Earth; and the gathering together of the waters called he Seas: and God saw that good.

11 And God said, Let the earth bring forth grass, the herb yielding seed, and the fruit tree yielding fruit after his kind, whose seed is in itself, upon the earth: and it was so. 12 And the earth brought forth grass, and herb yielding seed after his kind, and the tree yielding fruit, whose seed was in itself, after his kind: and God saw that it was good.

13 And the evening and the morning were the third day.

14 And God said, Let there be lights in the firmament of the heaven to divide the day from the night; and let them be for signs, and for seasons, and for days, and years:

15 And let them be for lights in the firmament of the heaven to give light upon the earth: and it was so.

16 And God made two great lights; the greater light to rule the day, and the lesser light to rule the night: he made the stars also.

17 And God set them in the firmament of the heaven to give light upon the earth,

18 And to rule over the day and over the night, and to divide the light from the darkness: and God saw that it was good.

19 And the evening and the morning were the fourth day.

20 And God said, Let the waters bring forth abundantly the moving creature that hath life, and fowl that may fly above the earth in the open firmament of heaven.

21 And God created great whales, and every living creature that moveth, which the waters brought forth abundantly, after their kind, and every winged fowl after his kind: and God saw that it was good.

22 And God blessed them, saying, Be fruitful, and multiply, and fill the waters in the seas, and let fowl multiply in the earth.

23 And the evening and the morning were the fifth day.

24 And God said, Let the earth bring forth the living creature after his kind, cattle, and creeping thing, and beast of the earth after his kind: and it was so.

25 And God made the beast of the earth after his kind, and cattle after their kind, and every thing that creepeth upon the earth after his kind: and God saw that it was good.

26 And God said, Let us make man in our image, after our likeness: and let them have dominion over the fish of the sea, and over the fowl of the air, and over the cattle, and over all the earth, and over every creeping thing that creepeth upon the earth.

27 So God created man in his own image, in the image of God created he him; male and female created he them.

28 And God blessed them, and God said unto them, Be fruitful, and multiply, and replenish the earth, and subdue it: and have dominion over the fish of the sea, and over the fowl of the air, and over every living thing that moveth upon the earth.

> 29 And God said, Behold, I have given you every herb bearing seed, which is upon the face of all the earth, and every tree, in the which is the fruit of a tree yielding seed; to you it shall be for meat.
>
> 30 And to every beast of the earth, and to every fowl of the air, and to every thing that creepeth upon the earth, wherein there is life, I have given every green herb for meat: and it was so.
>
> 31 And God saw every thing that he had made, and, behold, it was very good. And the evening and the morning were the sixth day.

I THINK I WAS ABOUT FORTY when I asked my mother for a Bible for Christmas. It was one of those pre-Christmas situations that happened every year. She would ask me what I wanted, and I, not having any idea, would rummage around in my brain until I came up with any tolerable answer. Most of the time it was something like a wallet, socks, or the always-needed new underwear. When Christmas came, I would act surprised and overly grateful for the perfect gift. That was our Christmas tradition. However, the year I turned forty, "Bible" just popped out of my mouth. I didn't need a Bible since there were so many online versions, but it was too late to think of another idea because my mother had already written "Bible" next to my name on her shopping list. It did give me a feeling of relief, though—at least for another year.

Not surprisingly, I initially thought the Bible would sit on my bookshelf and be forgotten. But there was something about reading an ancient text on paper rather than on a computer that helped me get into, can I say, a hallowed mood. There was just the Bible—no technology, no popups, and no audio prompts. Since that Christmas, I have read that Bible so often that many of the pages have come loose. In particular, not one page of the first eleven chapters of Genesis has a secure home. My Bible has become a loose-leaf folder. But as the pages lost their hold in the Bible, they took hold in me.

As I have said, I have not always read the Bible so passionately. For most of my life, I read, "In the beginning" the same way I spoke the Pledge of Allegiance, prayed the Lord's Prayer, or sang "The Star-Spangled Banner." I had memorized the first line of each of them from sheer repetition and then mumbled or hummed my way through the rest of each work. At that time, I also could only think of Genesis 1 as a literal description of the creation of the world and based my evaluation on that interpretation. Still, I knew I needed to do something different in order to get more from the text. With my new Bible, I forced myself to read each word of Genesis 1.

I studied each day, reading the passages over and over again until the pages fell out of my book, and an overall theme started to emerge. Genesis 1 became to me a poem describing everything I needed to know about faith. Day one tells about the creation and the purpose of faith. Days two through five tell some of the special qualities of faith. Day six shows that we as humans are the keepers of faith. And day seven finishes up with one final metaphor connecting Genesis 1 to the rest of the primeval history.

Let's go through the days of creation, one day at a time.

Day 1

Faith is the strength by which a shattered world shall emerge into the light.
—Helen Keller (1880–1968)[8]

> In the beginning God created the heaven and the earth. And the earth was without form, and void; and darkness was upon the face of the deep. And the Spirit of God moved upon the face of the waters. And God said, Let there be light: and there was light. And God saw the light, that it was good: and God divided the light from the darkness. And God called the light Day, and the darkness he called Night. And the evening and the morning were the first day. (Gen. 1:1–5)

ANY BOOK I HAVE EVER read to the end has started with an attention-grabber that compelled me to read more. For the better part of my life, reading Genesis 1 did not grab me. Even though I found the creation of the universe to be a fascinating topic and wanted to know more, I soon found Genesis turning into a mere list of things created. I really didn't care

8 ThinkExist.com Quotations. "Helen Keller quotes". ThinkExist.com Quotations Online 1 Oct. 2012. 19 Nov. 2012 <http://en.thinkexist.com/quotes/helen_keller/2.html>

that day five of creation was devoted to the making of birds and fish. Did it really matter on what day they were created? Why did the Bible waste its very first lines on documenting what happened on the seven days of creation? If I had written the Bible, I would have placed what happened on the days of creation back in an appendix, reserving the first chapter of the Bible for a *real* attention-grabber.

When I received the Bible from my mother, I decided to read it as though I had never read it before. That was when I asked myself if I was reading the text in the wrong way. I thought, *What do I want the Bible to tell me?* I wanted it to tell me about faith, so rather than giving up on the Bible again, I switched my thinking. I started asking myself, *If the beginning verses in the Bible are talking about faith, what are they saying?* That was the turning point in my understanding of the Bible. Reading Genesis 1:1–2:4a as a poem about faith captured my interest from the start, and I couldn't stop reading.

I was eager to see what the first book of the Bible had to say about faith; after all, it was *the* book on faith in the Western world. As I have said, I really never understood faith, so reading the chapter as a poem, with each line telling me something about faith, was entirely new and at first difficult. Every time I started to read, I would automatically slip back into thinking about the creation of the physical universe. But eventually, one verse at a time revealed to me its message about faith.

In terms of talking about faith, the Bible naturally starts with faith's creation and purpose. In the beginning, there was only darkness. Faith did not exist, so God created light. If Genesis was going to talk about faith, light is a good candidate for its metaphor. Faith, therefore, has existed since day one of creation. The creation poem goes on to tell us two more general characteristics of faith. The first characteristic is that faith is good. "And God saw the light, that it was good" (Gen. 1:4). The light, and therefore faith, is good. It is so good that Kierkegaard called it the *highest* good. "Faith is the highest passion in a human being. Many in every generation may not come that far, but none comes further."[9]

The second thing the poem reveals is that faith is separated from the darkness. "And God divided the light from the darkness. And God called the light Day, and the darkness he called Night. And the evening and the

9 ThinkExist.com Quotations. "Soren Kierkegaard quotes". ThinkExist.com Quotations Online 1 Oct. 2012. 19 Nov. 2012 <http://en.thinkexist.com/quotes/soren_kierkegaard/3.html>

morning were the first day" (Gen. 1:4b–5). If the light represents faith, we need to know what the darkness represents before we can see what this verse is trying to tell us. Here is where the *Blue Letter Bible* (BLB) first helped me to understand Genesis. (The BLB is a great online resource for looking up any fact you would ever want to know about many versions of the Bible.) The BLB tells us that the word *darkness* is used as a metaphor for "misery" and "adversity."[10] Since reading Genesis 1 as a poem is all about finding the metaphors, I think it is reasonable to assume that if faith is light, darkness is misery and adversity. Now we can tackle what these verses are trying to tell us.

In the beginning, God created something good called faith, and He separated it from all the misery and adversity of the rest of creation. But what was God really up to when He created faith and separated it from misery and adversity? Let's try to see it from God's point of view.

In the beginning, God saw only darkness (misery and adversity). He must have decided to do something about all this misery and adversity. Now I'm sure God had several options. Epicurus summarized God's problem. "Is God willing to prevent evil, but not able? Then he is not omnipotent. Is he able, but not willing? Then he is malevolent. Is he both able and willing? Then whence cometh evil?"[11]

God could have wiped out all the misery and made a perfect world, but He didn't. What He did was create a cure for this misery. He created faith and divided it from the misery and adversity. If He had created a perfectly good world, He wouldn't have needed to create faith, as we wouldn't have needed a cure if everything were perfect to begin with. But God thought it better to leave the misery alone and create faith as a special refuge set apart from all the misery and adversity of the world. In essence, the poem is telling us that there is something greater than a perfectly good world; it is an imperfect world plus faith. It is certainly a more interesting world with both good and evil. An all-good world would be at best boring, and I guess that would still be a bad thing.

---

10 Blue Letter Bible. "Dictionary and Word Search for '*darkness*' in the KJV." Blue Letter Bible. 1996–2012. November 6, 2012. http:// www.blueletterbible.org/search/translationResults.cfm?
Criteria=darkness&t=KJV.

11 ThinkExist.com Quotations. "Epicurus quotes". ThinkExist.com Quotations Online 1 Oct. 2012. 21 Nov. 2012 <http://en.thinkexist.com/quotes/epicurus/4.html>

Now we can see that God created faith as a wonderful gift to separate us from our misery and adversity. All we need to do if we can't tolerate our misery and adversity is find faith. Heinrich Heine, a German poet, directly captured this concept of faith being the solution to misery when he wrote, "Human misery is too great for men to do without faith."[12]

Wow! That's a lot of information about faith in five short verses. Now that grabs me! It tells me that faith is like light, and it is good. It is separate from the rest of my existence and was created to help me deal with all the misery and adversity in my life. But reading about day one of creation left me feeling faithless. I felt plenty of misery and adversity but very little refuge from them. Why did I see so much adversity and so little faith?

Where is all this faith that is supposed to help me? Who would I need to talk to? What did I need to do? The only thing that I knew for sure was that reading day one of creation as a metaphor for faith had given me more insight about faith than all my reading on the subject over the previous forty years. I was confident that if the Bible had started revealing to me what faith was, then it would surely reveal much more about faith, including where to find it. I would only have to keep reading.

12 ThinkExist.com Quotations. "Heinrich Heine quotes". ThinkExist.com Quotations Online 1 Oct. 2012. 19 Nov. 2012 <http://en.thinkexist.com/quotes/heinrich_heine/4.html>

Day 2

Faith is raising the sail of our little boat until it is caught up in the soft winds above and picks up speed, not from anything within itself, but from the vast resources of the universe around us.
—W. Ralph Ward (1911–1983)[13]

> And God said, Let there be a firmament in the midst of the waters, and let it divide the waters from the waters. And God made the firmament, and divided the waters which were under the firmament from the waters which were above the firmament: and it was so. And God called the firmament Heaven. And the evening and the morning were the second day. (Gen. 1:6–8)

The first day of creation was the beginning of a poem about faith, and it told me that God created faith to help me to separate myself from my adversities. But I certainly didn't feel that the faith in my life was strong enough to separate me from my adversities; in fact, I felt just the opposite, that the adversities in my life were taking up

13 QuoteDonkey.com. "W. Ralph Ward quotes". 2012. 19 Nov. 2012 http://www.quotesdonkey.com/author/w.-ralph-ward/

so much of my time that they prevented me from feeling more faith. So what was I missing here? Where was all the faith? If the second day of creation is going to tell me where faith is, then it will probably have something to do with the term *firmament,* since it is the central idea in these verses.

We know from day two of creation that the firmament is between the waters below, presumably the seas, and the waters above, presumably the clouds. From Genesis 1:17 and 1:20 we also know that the sun, moon, and stars are in the firmament and fowl fly in the firmament. The only concept I know of that includes all of these definitions is the sky. From our perspective, the sky separates the clouds from the seas; the sun, the moon, and the stars are in the sky, and the birds fly in the sky. With that definition, we too live in the sky—the sky that is immediately above the earth. So what does this imply about where faith is?

I think it is telling us that faith is everywhere, but it is invisible, just like the sky. Even though it is right in front of us, we cannot see it. For God, the sky was not too high and not too low; it was just right for faith, as Goldilocks might have said. God even called this firmament *heaven.*[14]

> And God called the firmament Heaven ... (Gen. 1:8)

This metaphor also tells us that from our perspective, faith is seemingly invisible, just like the air in the sky. How should I understand this part of the metaphor? Over the years, I have come across several quotes that help address this question.

> The kingdom of the father is spread out upon the earth, and men do not see it.
>
> —Gospel of Thomas (c. 200)[15]

14 This implies that through faith one exists in heaven. Whether this heaven continues after death is not addressed, and as far as I am concerned, it is not an important issue. We should all be seeking heaven and therefore faith while we are alive.

15 The Gospel According to Thomas. James M. Robinson, ed., *The Nag Hammadi Library,* revised edition. HarperCollins, San Francisco, 1990.

> It is the heart which perceives God and not the reason. That is what faith is: God perceived by the heart, not by the reason.
>
> —Blaise Pascal (1623–1662)[16]

> The way to see Faith is to shut the Eye of Reason.
>
> —Benjamin Franklin (1706–1790)[17]

By putting these quotes together, it became clear to me that my ordinary thought processes, my thinking, and my wisdom would not help me see faith. Faith is invisible to reason but not to the heart. Just like the sky, we can't really see it, but we are sure glad it's there. Like I have said, it was easy for me to see all the adversity of my life, but to perceive God with my heart—what was that all about?

To begin to see with my heart, I started in the only place I knew of to escape from my adversity: the bathtub. In the bathtub, I was not participating in all the commotion of the world. At first I found bathtubs to be great places to study during school. No one would bother me for at least an hour. After I finished school, I continued to find sanctuary in my time in the bathtub. I would take a large book into the bathroom, as if I were going to do some heavy reading, but most of the time I would just stretch out in the tub and unwind. I would keep the hot water running at barely a trickle, with the sound of the water adding to the experience. If I spent too much time in the bathtub, I would usually hear a knock on the door and a teasing voice checking to see if I had shriveled up. In the bathtub I felt safe, I felt warm, and I felt good—very good.

The bathtub that I had when I received my Bible for Christmas was an extra-deep one made in 1926. It had been refinished several times but looked as good as new. This is where I started reading that Bible and where the pages fell out. Luckily none of those pages fell into the bathwater, like so many of my textbooks did during school. The Bible's pages stayed right with me

16 ThinkExist.com Quotations. "Blaise Pascal quotes". ThinkExist.com Quotations Online 1 Oct. 2012. 19 Nov. 2012 <http://en.thinkexist.com/quotes/Blaise_Pascal/4.html>

17 ThinkExist.com Quotations. "Benjamin Franklin quotes". ThinkExist.com Quotations Online 1 Oct. 2012. 19 Nov. 2012 <http://en.thinkexist.com/quotes/Benjamin_Franklin/4.html>

between the waters below in the tub and the waters above in the showerhead. It became my firmament, my heaven. I believe that my heart might have even started to perceive God. The bathtub became my own personal symbol of faith, as important to me as a cross, a star, or a crescent was to others. I would even say that my faith was cast iron. If I was in a stressful situation, all I would have to do was imagine myself back in my tub with the water trickling and I felt better.

What day two of creation was telling me was that faith can be found everywhere, but we can't see it with our power of reason, our wisdom. Faith can be found in a church, a forest, and yes, even a bathtub. That being said, I'm quite sure that I would be disturbing many people's faith if I brought my bathtub to church with me or invited anyone to share faith at my place of worship.

Still, I knew that there had to be more because my bathtub faith certainly wasn't strong enough for many adverse situations. I had sampled faith, but what was the next step that I needed to take to get more? I hoped the creation poem was up to the challenge of helping me to experience a much more profound faith and a peaceful heart. Who was I kidding? I trusted that the Bible was up to the challenge; but was I?

> Faith indeed tells what the senses do not tell, but not the contrary of what they see. It is above them and not contrary to them.
>
> —Blaise Pascal (1623–1662)[18]

18 ThinkExist.com Quotations. "Blaise Pascal quotes". ThinkExist.com Quotations Online 1 Oct. 2012. 19 Nov. 2012 <http://en.thinkexist.com/quotes/Blaise_Pascal/3.html>

DAY 3

Seeds of faith are always within us; sometimes it takes a crisis to nourish and encourage their growth.
—Susan L. Taylor (1946–)[19]

And God said, Let the waters under the heaven be gathered together unto one place, and let the dry land appear: and it was so. And God called the dry land Earth; and the gathering together of the waters called the Seas: and God saw that it was good. And God said, Let the earth bring forth grass, the herb yielding seed, and the fruit tree yielding fruit after his kind, whose seed is in itself, upon the earth: and it was so. And the earth brought forth grass, and herb yielding seed after his kind, and the tree yielding fruit, whose seed was in itself, after his kind: and God saw that it was good. And the evening and the morning were the third day. (Gen. 1:9–13)

DAY TWO TOLD US THAT faith is everywhere but we can't see it. We cannot see faith with our rational brains; we must use our hearts. But

19 ThinkExist.com Quotations. "Susan Taylor quotes". ThinkExist.com Quotations Online 1 Oct. 2012. 19 Nov. 2012 <http://en.thinkexist.com/quotes/susan_taylor/>

how do we use our hearts to "see" faith? Day three of creation gives us the answer by using an analogy of seeds.

> And the earth brought forth grass, and herb yielding seed after his kind, and the tree yielding fruit, whose seed was in itself, after his kind: and God saw that it was good. (Gen. 1:12)

All plants have seeds in them, and by analogy, we too have human seeds in us. But the Bible isn't talking about our biological seeds; it's telling us that we have seeds of faith in us. If we think about it, we have all kinds of seeds in us. If we are doubtful, we have doubtful seeds; if we are afraid, we have fearful seeds; and if we are boastful, we have boastful seeds. Whatever our brains are thinking or feeling, those are the seeds we are planting. The heart, not the head, sees a different kind of seed; even in the worst of situations, it sees the seeds of faith. We have the choice to sow the seeds of our heads or our hearts.

For instance, if our heads decide to walk around in a repulsive mood, then we are going to sow repulsive seeds in our lives. Those seeds will germinate, grow, and multiply. We, of course, will surround ourselves with prissiness, and that is how we will see the world and the world will see us. So if we want to see the world of faith, we must sow the seeds of faith, which conveniently are already in us. Sometimes it may be hard to find the small seeds of faith in life, especially when the repulsive weeds take over. To understand what the seeds of faith look like, I'd like to share an example of a friend who has sown his faith seeds regardless of his situation.

A few years ago, I was talking to my friend about seeing the world with the heart and not the head. A couple of weeks later, he came back to me and told me that he had changed his thinking from his head to his heart when reading his favorite Bible verse. He told me that the verse was:

> Delight thyself also in the LORD and He shall give thee the desires of thine heart. (Ps. 37:4)

My friend said that he had always interpreted this verse to mean that if he delighted in the Lord, the Lord would reward him with everything he wanted. He told me that our discussion on how to see things—not with the eye of reason but with the heart—had helped him reinterpret this verse. He told me, "If I delight in the Lord, the Lord will take away the desires I already selfishly have and will give me the desires that He wants me to have." Furthermore, he told me that most of his own desires, once fulfilled, didn't give him all that much happiness anyway, and he welcomed the idea of what God wanted for him. All I said back to him was "That's it."

His life changed forever because he had found a seed of faith and planted it. His seed of faith was a tiny switch in how he had always read his favorite verse. By rejoicing in the Lord, he found that his true desires were not his own but were given to him by the Lord. My friend has found that seeing the seed of faith in any situation produces benefits far beyond our expectations. To this day, he tells me that his realization of a different way of understanding his favorite verse has continued to make him a better father and husband. He begrudgingly told me that he was even a better ex-husband. He qualified that by saying that he still needed to find many more seeds to help him with that relationship.

In the example, once discovered, the seeds of faith changed my friend's life. It literally took away his suffering and gave him a more peaceful heart. It is not easy to find the seeds of faith in us; it takes real work, usually under unpleasant circumstances. One way I have found to see these seeds is to ask the question, "What message is God trying to send me in this situation that will help me to have a better life?" My friend had a much better life and a more peaceful heart when he realized that he would prefer that the desires of his heart be directed by the Lord rather than by himself. His desires didn't give him lasting happiness anyway, so he wasn't losing anything. Once my friend found his first seed of faith, it became much easier to keep finding them in all aspects of his life, and I'm sure one day he will find the seeds of faith he needs for his relationship with his ex-wife.

Once I realized that finding the seeds of faith was the first step in the process of letting faith enrich one's life, especially in less than desirable situations, all I wanted to do was look for those seeds. Likewise, I wanted to tell everyone else in my life about this discovery. My friends got sick of me asking them about their seeds of faith, especially when they were in bad moods. If they were in a bad mood and I came bouncing up to them asking them about their seeds of faith, depending on their familiarity with expletives, most of them would somehow tell me to mind my own business. They also told me that I was becoming obnoxious with my "seeds of faith" questions. I was sure day four of creation would teach me how to moderate my quest.

> If fear is cultivated it will become stronger, if faith is cultivated it will achieve mastery.
>
> —John Paul Jones (1747–1792)[20]

20 ThinkExist.com Quotations. "John Paul Jones quotes". ThinkExist.com Quotations Online 1 Oct. 2012. 19 Nov. 2012 <http://en.thinkexist.com/quotes/john_paul_jones/>

Day 4

The Bible shows the way to go to heaven, not the way the heavens go.
—Galileo Galilei (1564–1642)[21]

And God said, Let there be lights in the firmament of the heaven to divide the day from the night; and let them be for signs, and for seasons, and for days, and years: And let them be for lights in the firmament of the heaven to give light upon the earth: and it was so. And God made two great lights; the greater light to rule the day, and the lesser light to rule the night: he made the stars also. And God set them in the firmament of the heaven to give light upon the earth, And to rule over the day and over the night, and to divide the light from the darkness: and God saw that it was good. And the evening and the morning were the fourth day. (Gen. 1:14–19)

We already know that light symbolizes faith from day one of creation, so is day four of creation restating this, or is it trying to

21 ThinkExist.com Quotations. "Galileo Galilei quotes". ThinkExist.com Quotations Online 1 Oct. 2012. 19 Nov. 2012 <http://en.thinkexist.com/quotes/galileo_galilei/>

tell us something new about faith? We also know that day three told us that faith is like tiny seeds that we can sow; these seeds grow and give us a more peaceful heart. Sure, we need to keep finding new seeds of faith, but the next step in discovering what faith is all about is to understand how we are to express it. The fourth day is telling us we are not to try to recruit others to join us, especially if they don't want to. This is what I wanted to do after discovering some of my seeds of faith. The next step is just to let our faith shine from within and see how it improves not only our lives but the lives of everybody around us too. Everybody will see a change in us; some will respond to our new glow and some will not. It is not up to us what others do. It is just up to us to let our peaceful hearts shine forth.

Now, God made two great lights, the sun and moon, as examples of how we should shine. The sun and moon shine day after day, season after season, and year after year. They don't hold back, they don't negotiate, and they don't withdraw.

> Someday perhaps the inner light will shine forth from us, and then we'll need no other light.
>
> —Johann Wolfgang von Goethe (1749–1832)[22]

> People are like stained-glass windows. They sparkle and shine when the sun is out, but when the darkness sets in their true beauty is revealed only if there is light from within.
>
> —Elisabeth Kübler-Ross (1926–2004)[23]

> Faith is like electricity. You can't see it, but you can see the light.
>
> —Anonymous[24]

22 ThinkExist.com Quotations. "Johann Wolfgang von Goethe quotes". ThinkExist.com Quotations Online 1 Oct. 2012. 19 Nov. 2012 <http://en.thinkexist.com/quotes/johann_wolfgang_von_goethe/10.html>

23 ThinkExist.com Quotations. "Elisabeth Kubler-Ross quotes". ThinkExist.com Quotations Online 1 Oct. 2012. 19 Nov. 2012 <http://en.thinkexist.com/quotes/elisabeth_kubler-ross/>

24 ThinkExist.com Quotations. "electricityquotes". ThinkExist.com Quotations Online 1 Oct. 2012. 21 Nov. 2012 <http://en.thinkexist.com/quotes/with/keyword/electricity/>

Let me give an example of how I radiated faith, and at the time I didn't even know I was doing it. During summer vacations from college and medical school, I was expected to work to help pay my tuition. One summer I found a job as a nurse's aide on the 3:00 to 11:00 shift at a nearby nursing home. Now don't get me wrong, I had plenty of fun on that job, since I was the only male employee at the time and had more than enough attention, but I was also assigned most of the male patients and mainly had the duty of getting them ready for bed. One particular gentleman named John always requested me, and I knew why. Most—no, every evening after supper, he had diarrhea. I don't know if it was his medication, but they had tried everything to stop it; however, anything that worked, worked too well. This was also before the time of Depends undergarments, so we just had to use extra rubber sheets on his bed. He would never tell the nurse when he had diarrhea; he just told her that he was fine until I got there.

Every night we would have our routine. I would help him to the bathroom, draw some warm, soapy water, and clean him from top to bottom—mainly bottom. Then I would help him to bed. The nightly diarrhea had caused a very irritated area, and what made each night worse was that John had a tendency to swear when he was in pain. He definitely showed that he was in pain every night. Oh, I forgot to say that I would also make sure that not only the bathroom door was closed but also the room door, to give an extra bit of insulation between his mouth and the other residents. Once the nightly ritual was over, John was ready for bed. Once in bed, John would give me the best smile he could muster and wave goodnight.

The other aides I worked with couldn't stand John and were happy to see me coming to work, knowing that he would be assigned to me for at least that evening. They also couldn't understand why it didn't bother me to work with John. Was I gullible or just passive not to demand that the misery of taking care of John be shared among all the aides? Well, at that time I couldn't explain it, but I know now that throughout that summer I was blessed with a peaceful heart and somehow I showed it to others. I was shining, and I didn't even know it. All the other aids saw it, but most of them interpreted it as a negative—that I didn't stand up for myself in the face of an obvious inequity. But I wasn't suffering from any inequity; I felt good about helping John. Why would I think it was unfair? As I look back on that situation, I know it was faith that not only made my job pleasant for me but also gave me a peaceful heart.

Once I saw that I must have been radiating faith during my nursing home experience, it changed the way I envisioned faith and convinced me that I had been wasting my time trying to study faith to see what it was all about. My real quest was not simply to understand faith but just to radiate it. I was radiating faith in the nursing home before I knew what I was doing. In the same way, the sun, moon, and stars are unaware that they radiate light; they just do it. Interestingly, once I gave up trying to understand faith, it became a lot easier to see faith being radiated from others.

Once we start to radiate faith, we change forever, just like my friend after he reinterpreted his favorite Bible verse. People will invariably notice a change in us, but their reaction might not be what is expected. Just like my friends in the nursing home, many people will never see the radiance of faith, and that's okay. We're not radiating faith for others to see; we're doing it for the benefit it gives us, the relief from misery and adversity in our own lives. If I think about it, I'm sure that many of my fellow nursing aides were radiating faith themselves, just not when it came to working with John. Don't get me wrong—when somebody else does see faith in us or we see it in them, it's a reason for celebration, just as I celebrated with my friend when he shared his reinterpretation of Psalm 37:4.

Day four of creation is telling us not to bother with trying to see or understand faith; as long as we radiate it, we will enjoy its benefits. With faith, we are the lights in the firmament. Day five of creation gives us metaphors to tell us that we should enjoy the ride that faith takes us on. Faith is abundant, like the fish in the sea, and will help us flow around any obstacles in life, but we must remember that we cannot steer or direct faith as we would like.

> As your faith is strengthened you will find that there is no longer the need to have a sense of control, that things will flow as they will, and that you will flow with them, to your great delight and benefit.
>
> —Emmanuel Teney[25]

25 ThinkExist.com Quotations. "Emmanuel Teney quotes". ThinkExist.com Quotations Online 1 Oct. 2012. 19 Nov. 2012 <http://en.thinkexist.com/quotes/emmanuel_teney/>

Day 5

Faith is not something to grasp, it is a state to grow into.
—Mahatma Gandhi (1869–1948)[26]

And God said, Let the waters bring forth abundantly the moving creature that hath life, and fowl that may fly above the earth in the open firmament of heaven. And God created great whales, and every living creature that moveth, which the waters brought forth abundantly, after their kind, and every winged fowl after his kind: and God saw that it was good. And God blessed them, saying, Be fruitful, and multiply, and fill the waters in the seas, and let fowl multiply in the earth. And the evening and the morning were the fifth day. (Gen. 1:20–23)

Day five tells us that faith is abundant and multiplies in the world. Faith swims, flies, and flows through our lives. I think this is also a subtle warning not to hold on to faith and think it is something to possess, control, or direct. If we hold a fish still in the water it will drown; if we cage

26 ThinkExist.com Quotations. "Mahatma Gandhi quotes". ThinkExist.com Quotations Online 1 Oct. 2012. 21 Nov. 2012 <http://en.thinkexist.com/quotes/mahatma_gandhi/10.html>

a bird, it will be unable to fly. Likewise, if we restrain faith, it will wither. To understand this metaphor, I remember a time in high school when my family moved to a new house in town. I grew up in Portage, Michigan, where "in town" meant that the houses were on lots rather than acres. My parents, having three teenagers, thought that it would be better to be closer to school and friends rather than way out in the country.

Moving gave me the opportunity to express one of my other interests: gardening. I now had a yard that I could have a real garden in, rather than just mowing an acre of weeds and cutting the overgrown lilacs to the ground. About a mile away from our new house was a house that had the most beautiful island perennial border that I had ever seen. What added to my awe was that I never saw anybody working on it. I would go out of my way to and from school just to watch the garden change through the season. I loved that garden just for the experience of seeing it bloom; it was radiant. I also studied it with the intent of making my own garden at the new house. It would make our yard a place where others would pause and hopefully feel what I had felt. But it never worked; no matter how hard I tried, it fell short, and it frustrated me to no end.

How could that gardener who was never present create such an incredible garden when I worked overtime and failed? I was trying to possess that garden for my own purpose, and in the end, I even spoiled the experience I had with the original border. In my desire to acquire that garden for myself, I had destroyed everything I loved about it. My point is that no one can possess faith or it will die in us, just like the fish in the sea if we hold them still. Similarly, faith will forget how to soar, just like the fowl of the firmament if we cage them. At the very best, faith abundantly flows through us into the world, and that itself is the benefit.

> Faith is daring the soul to go beyond what it can see.
>
> —William Newton Clark (1841–1912)[27]

27 ThinkExist.com Quotations. "William Newton Clarke quotes". ThinkExist.com Quotations Online 1 Oct. 2012. 21 Nov. 2012 <http://en.thinkexist.com/quotes/william_newton_clarke/>

Day 6

We must be willing to let go of the life we planned so as to have the life that is waiting for us.
—Joseph Campbell (1904–1987)[28]

And God said, Let the earth bring forth the living creature after his kind, cattle, and creeping thing, and beast of the earth after his kind: and it was so. And God made the beast of the earth after his kind, and cattle after their kind, and every thing that creepeth upon the earth after his kind: and God saw that it was good. And God said, Let us make man in our image, after our likeness: and let them have dominion over the fish of the sea, and over the fowl of the air, and over the cattle, and over all the earth, and over every creeping thing that creepeth upon the earth. So God created man in his own image, in the image of God created he him; male and female created he them. And God blessed them, and God said unto them, Be fruitful, and multiply, and replenish the earth, and subdue it: and have dominion over the fish of the sea, and over the fowl of the air, and

28 ThinkExist.com Quotations. "Joseph Campbell quotes". ThinkExist.com Quotations Online 1 Oct. 2012. 19 Nov. 2012 <http://en.thinkexist.com/quotes/joseph_campbell/>

> over every living thing that moveth upon the earth. And God said, Behold, I have given you every herb bearing seed, which is upon the face of all the earth, and every tree, in the which is the fruit of a tree yielding seed; to you it shall be for meat. And to every beast of the earth, and to every fowl of the air, and to every thing that creepeth upon the earth, wherein there is life, I have given every green herb for meat: and it was so. And God saw every thing that he had made, and, behold, it was very good. And the evening and the morning were the sixth day. (Gen. 1:24–31)

To summarize Genesis 1 so far: The first day of creation tells us that faith is good and separates us from all the misery and adversity of our lives. Faith is invisible to rational human thinking, but we can find seeds of faith in everything we do and everything that happens to us. It is the seeds that will make us a better person and help us grow in faith. Once faith starts to grow in us, it produces its own light within us. When it starts to shine, we must radiate it freely and abundantly into the world to reap faith's benefit. Day 6 of the creation poem tells us that this way of living is "very good." This is the way the world has been set up, and it will work at its best if we follow these instructions. The Lord God blessed us with this gift, but we can do with it what we will since we have dominion over the world. We were created in the Lord God's image; therefore, we can also create things. We can try, on our own, to find happiness and comfort from all the misery and adversity in life. Our rational brains can try to come up with a system better than the one presented in Genesis 1, and we are free to try it out, but the Bible isn't recommending that course. Let me give an example of how I decided to try it my way and the subsequent results.

It was a busy time in my life; I had just started a new job. Actually it was my first job in my chosen profession as an allergist, and I was fresh out of my fellowship. My wife and I were trying to have a baby, and it was not happening naturally. I was also diagnosed with a rare form of cancer called a sarcoma that luckily I was "cured" from. To top it all off, my mother called in the midst of all this and told me that my father had laryngeal cancer and needed a tracheotomy. He wasn't expected to live more than a year. Despite all that was going wrong, it was the best year of my life, but once again, I didn't know it at the time.

Now besides being the family gardener, I was, for as long as I can remember, the one who kept the family together. Whether I needed to take on that role or not was a matter of debate, but I did take my job very seriously. Was my family a typical family with all the usual clashes? I don't know, but I had this vision of what an ideal family should be, and I was always trying to have my family fit that ideal. I would spend a lot of time trying to have everyone get along, even when it was none of my business, and I was always planning family get-togethers. Of course, just like my failed efforts to grow the perfect garden, I had unrealistic goals for my family too.

When my father developed cancer, the whole family rallied around him, and for that last year of his life, everyone was remarkably happy, especially my dad. I could see it in his eyes. I don't know if he found faith, but he sure had a more peaceful heart that last year of his life. One would have thought that I too would have had a good year because my whole family was together and happy, but I did not. Inside, I was angry at my father's cancer, but I was not because it was going to kill him. I was mad at the cancer for doing what I couldn't do all those years. I worked all my life to bring the family together, and it never succeeded. Cancer brought my family together, and I resented it. I was trying to create my own happiness with my own self-will, not with faith.

After my dad died, it took a while, but I finally recognized that I had gotten exactly what I had wanted; my family was together and happy. I had worked, worried, and whined all those years to bring my family together. But all I really had to do was to wait to find the seed of faith in my father's cancer, a terrible illness that, even though it was negative, brought my family together. It was literally the last time my family had a chance to be together and to be happy. Everyone knew it except me, and they jumped at the opportunity. At that time, I was still stuck in trying to do things my way, but I see it differently now. When I recognized the seed of faith in that situation, even though it was years after the events, my heart became a lot more peaceful.

Day seven of creation concludes the creation poem about faith by telling us that the peace and rest we get from faith is out of this world ... and more!

> Faith consists in believing when it is beyond the power of reason to believe.
>
> —Voltaire (1674–1778)[29]

29 ThinkExist.com Quotations. "Voltaire quotes". ThinkExist.com Quotations Online 1 Oct. 2012. 19 Nov. 2012 <http://en.thinkexist.com/quotes/voltaire/6.html>

Day 7

Nothing in life is more wonderful than faith—the one great moving force which we can neither weigh in the balance nor test in the crucible.
—William Osler (1849–1919)[30]

> Thus the heavens and the earth were finished, and all the host of them. And on the seventh day God ended his work which he had made; and he rested on the seventh day from all his work which he had made. And God blessed the seventh day, and sanctified it: because that in it he had rested from all his work which God created and made. These are the generations of the heavens and of the earth when they were created. (Gen. 2:1–4)

Now we have reached the final day of creation. At first I thought it was very peculiar to have day seven of creation written in Genesis 2, not in chapter 1 with the rest of the creation poem. But because of this placement, it can be thought of as acting as both the conclusion to the creation poem and the introduction to the second chapter of Genesis. By doing so,

30 ThinkExist.com Quotations. "William Osler quotes". ThinkExist.com Quotations Online 1 Oct. 2012. 19 Nov. 2012 <http://en.thinkexist.com/quotes/william_osler/5.html>

it connects the two chapters and tells us that even though the chapters look and sound completely different, Genesis 2 will continue to talk about faith. We'll first look at day seven as the conclusion of the creation poem.

Day seven ends the creation poem by telling us the ultimate purpose of God's creation—of faith—is to find rest. But this is not an ordinary physical or even emotional rest. It is a spiritual rest, not bound by our concepts of space or time. The Bible uses the text itself to tell us that it is outside the bounds of space and time. In terms of space, since the creation poem is written in the first chapter of Genesis and day seven is outside of that "space" (being found in the second chapter), it seems reasonable that the resting place that we are talking about is not bound by any spatial limitation.

In terms of time, day seven does not follow the format of the other six days of creation when they end in the phrase: "And the evening and the morning were the ____ day."

The seventh day, as far as we can tell, never ends, and this makes it outside the limits of time too. What a wonderful image, resting with God forever outside the bounds of time and physical realities and limitations. This surely sounds like the heaven that the other days of creation allude to. We can see that as a conclusion to the creation poem, day seven hits the mark by telling us that the ultimate resting place for us is in faith. Heaven and faith are one and the same.

At this point, I'd like to reiterate how much I've gotten out of reading Genesis 1–2:4a as a poem about faith. Exploring each metaphor and applying it to my life situations has filled my life with faith. My bathtub faith has grown, and I now feel that for anything I need to deal with in my life, I can apply these principles of faith and find a peaceful heart. I could not imagine ever again limiting this poem to a literal description of the creation of the world. What a wonderful gift I've been given to have faith radiating in my life.

If we turn now to reading the last day of creation as the introduction to the second chapter of Genesis, we see a whole new story beginning. By sharing day seven, we can see that the two chapters share the same message. As the end of the creation poem, day seven tells us that faith is the ultimate resting place for God, the main character in Genesis 1. God rested from all the work He had done in creating faith. Since the seventh day of creation also beings chapter 2, we must also assume that faith is the ultimate resting place for Adam, the main character in the second creation story. Genesis 2 again uses the motif of the creation of the world with its rivers, vegetation, animals, and a special garden to represent what work will be required of Adam and every human to have the spiritual rest found on the seventh day of the first creation story. We will discuss these metaphors more in the following chapter.

> The attitude of faith is to let go and become open to the truth, whatever it might turn out to be ... The attitude of faith is the very opposite of clinging to belief, of holding on.
>
> —Alan Watts (1915–1973)[31]

31 Alan Watts. BrainyQuote.com, Xplore Inc, 2012. http://www.brainyquote.com/quotes/quotes/a/alanwatts252964.html, accessed November 21, 2012.

On a long journey of human life, faith is the best of companions; it is the best refreshment on the journey; and it is the greatest property.
—Siddhārtha Gautama (c. 563 BCE–483 BCE)[32]

Genesis 2

1 Thus the heavens and the earth were finished, and all the
host of them. 2 And on the seventh day God ended his work
which he had made; and he rested on the seventh day from
all his work which he had made.

3 And God blessed the seventh day, and sanctified it: because that in it he had rested from all his work which God created and made.

4 These are the generations of the heavens and of the earth when they were created, in the day that the LORD God made the earth and the heavens,

5 And every plant of the field before it was in the earth, and every herb of the field before it grew: for the LORD God had not caused it to rain upon the earth, and there was not a man to till the ground.

6 But there went up a mist from the earth, and watered the whole face of the ground.

7 And the LORD God formed man of the dust of the ground, and breathed into his nostrils the breath of life; and man became a living soul.

8 And the LORD God planted a garden eastward in Eden; and there he put the man whom he had formed.

9 And out of the ground made the LORD God to grow every tree that is pleasant to the sight, and good for food;

32 ThinkExist.com Quotations. "Buddha quotes". ThinkExist.com Quotations Online 1 Oct. 2012. 21 Nov. 2012 <http://en.thinkexist.com/quotes/buddha/10.html>

the tree of life also in the midst of the garden, and the tree of knowledge of good and evil.

10 And a river went out of Eden to water the garden; and from thence it was parted, and became into four heads.

11 The name of the first is Pison: that is it which compasseth the whole land of Havilah, where there is gold;

12 And the gold of that land is good: there is bdellium and the onyx stone.

13 And the name of the second river is Gihon: the same is it that compasseth the whole land of Ethiopia.

14 And the name of the third river is Hiddekel: that is it which goeth toward the east of Assyria. And the fourth river is Euphrates.

15 And the LORD God took the man, and put him into the garden of Eden to dress it and to keep it.

16 And the LORD God commanded the man, saying, Of every tree of the garden thou mayest freely eat:

17 But of the tree of the knowledge of good and evil, thou shalt not eat of it: for in the day that thou eatest thereof thou shalt surely die.

18 And the LORD God said, It is not good that the man should be alone; I will make him an help meet for him.

19 And out of the ground the LORD God formed every beast of the field, and every fowl of the air; and brought them unto Adam to see what he would call them: and whatsoever Adam called every living creature, that was the name thereof.

20 And Adam gave names to all cattle, and to the fowl of the air, and to every beast of the field; but for Adam there was not found an help meet for him.

21 And the LORD God caused a deep sleep to fall upon Adam, and he slept: and he took one of his ribs, and closed up the flesh instead thereof;

22 And the rib, which the LORD God had taken from man, made he a woman, and brought her unto the man.

23 And Adam said, This is now bone of my bones, and flesh of my flesh: she shall be called Woman, because she was taken out of Man.

24 Therefore shall a man leave his father and his mother, and shall cleave unto his wife: and they shall be one flesh.

25 And they were both naked, the man and his wife, and were not ashamed.

THERE ARE TWO THINGS THAT we immediately notice when reading Genesis 2. The first is that the stories of Genesis 1 and 2 overlap, and the second is that they are both creation stories. The overlap of the two creation stories acts to tie them together and tells us that we should read them as a pair; we cannot truly understand one without the other. But there are too many contradictory messages between the two stories to let us think this understanding will be easy. For instance, there is a reversal of the order of the creation of man and the animals in the two accounts.[33] How can both versions be true if we are talking about the same creation? How can we reconcile this discrepancy and understand what the Bible is trying to tell us about faith as a whole?

The easiest way to reconcile the differences in these stories is to assume that they are talking about the same thing from a different point of view, as

33 Genesis 1 has the animals created before or on day six, just before the creation of man. Genesis 2 has man created first and then the animals.

much of the Bible does. I believe one of the opening verses in Genesis 2 is telling us about this change in perspective:

> These are the generations of the heavens and of the earth when they were created, in the day that the LORD God made the earth and the heavens. (Gen. 2:4)

Isn't it interesting that there is a reversal in the "heaven and earth" wording order within the same verse? I think this implies that the Bible is presenting the same topic from the exact opposite point of view. Remembering that Genesis 1 is a poem using God's creation of the physical world as a metaphor for the creation of faith, it would seem logical that Genesis 2 is using the creation of the physical world again as a metaphor for faith from somebody else's point of view, namely Adam's view or the human perspective. It tells us what the human view of faith will be.

We already know from the sixth day of creation written about in Genesis 1 that God wants humans to have the benefits of His greatest creation, faith. But having these benefits is a great responsibility. It means that we can and must decide whether faith will be the most important thing in our lives, the least important thing in our lives, or a place somewhere ambivalently in-between. Genesis 2 tells us how to best take care of faith or how we can create a life that fully includes faith. Before we discuss these instructions, let's review the major events and characters of the creation account.

As we have discussed, the story of Genesis 2 opens on day seven of the first creation story, with God resting from all His work. The story then has a flashback to before creation and starts with the rising of the mist and the making of man. Adam, the first man, is made out of the dust of the ground and the breath of the Lord God. The Lord God then planted the garden of Eden and placed Adam in it. Adam's job was to be the keeper of the garden. The garden included a river and two special trees. The river watered the garden and then divided into four rivers that flowed out of the garden in all directions. The two trees were named the tree of life and the tree of the knowledge of good and evil.

But the garden was not a perfect place. It was not without some dangers. For instance, the Lord God told Adam that if he ate from the tree of the knowledge of good and evil, he would die. I can imagine that Adam thought to himself, *If eating some fruit will kill me, what other perils will await me in this so-called paradise?* The garden was also imperfect because it lacked animals and a mate for Adam. The Lord God therefore created animals for Adam to name and a woman for Adam to join him as a mate. The woman was found to be a good partner for Adam, and they lived together in the garden without shame. Things had become almost perfect, but there was still that deadly tree in the midst of the garden that Adam would have to deal with. Why had the Lord God so vehemently warned Adam not to eat of that tree? Now that we have reviewed the storyline, let's explore what Genesis 2 is trying to tell us about creating a life involving faith and how it answers Adam's questions.

The introductory verses of Genesis 2, even though they are still part of the Genesis 1 poem, tell us that the highest achievement in life is to be able to rest with God on the seventh day. The Bible also uses Genesis 1 as a template to show us how we should live our lives. God worked for six days creating faith, and then He rested in it. We too should work as the keeper of the garden of Eden, and then we too will be able to rest with God in faith. I don't think the Bible means to imply that we must work for exactly six days and then rest for exactly one day. Sometimes we need a little more rest and sometimes we need a little more work. Either way is fine as long as we understand the pattern.

The Bible makes it easy for us to understand just exactly what our work is by using the image of a garden. The only instructions given to Adam were to be the garden's keeper and not to eat from one of its trees. By placing Adam in a preformed garden, the Lord God made it clear that everything was already set up the way that the Lord God wanted it to be. It was not up to Adam to change things, only to take care of the way they were. The Lord God had given Adam two gifts to make this happen. The first gift was faith, and it was symbolized by the tree of life. The tree of life was there to remind Adam that he could have comfort and rest, just as God had on the seventh day of creation. The second gift, symbolized by the tree of the knowledge of good and evil, can be seen as wisdom; it was given to Adam to remind him that it takes wisdom to know how to do the work of being the keeper of the garden. It may at first sound funny that the tree of the knowledge of good and evil was a gift from the Lord God, since it has such a bad reputation as being the source of Adam's "fall," but we must remember that this interpretation is only one of many possible understandings. At least for now, let's be open to the possibility that the tree of the knowledge of good and evil could be a good thing. After all, God said that everything He created was good. Besides, I can't imagine that God would think there is anything wrong with us using our wisdom if we use it primarily to take care of the garden of Eden. Using different terms for wisdom, Sophocles and Galileo seem to agree.

> Reason is God's crowning gift to man.
>
> —Sophocles (497/6–406/5 BCE)[34]

> I do not feel obliged to believe that the same God who endowed us with sense, reason, and intellect has intended us to forgo their use.
>
> —Galileo Galilei (1564–1642)[35]

By giving us both faith and wisdom, the Lord God is telling us that they work as a team. Wisdom must work to keep a garden safe and secure in our lives, and faith will comfort us from all the work we must do to keep the garden. At first we may have thought that being a garden's keeper would be a "piece of cake," that the Lord God has created a beautiful garden for us and all we have to do is maintain it. But it is all too human to not leave well enough alone. No matter how good things are going, don't we all have a little voice in our heads telling us that things can be better? Remembering that the garden of Eden was not a perfect place to begin with (remember, God told Adam he actually had to work in the garden), why shouldn't we try our hand at improving it? Well, for one reason—the Lord God does not want us to rearrange His garden; it is just the way He wants it already. That being said, it seems to me that keeping the garden is easy when everything in our lives is going well and when we agree with the way the Lord God has arranged things in our life. It becomes another story when problems arise or we don't like the Lord God's plans for us. When the world gives us a little misery and adversity, we need all the wisdom we can muster to remember that the care of our garden is our first priority.

---

34 ThinkExist.com Quotations. "Sophocles quotes". ThinkExist.com Quotations Online 1 Oct. 2012. 20 Nov. 2012 <http://en.thinkexist.com/quotes/sophocles/6.html>

35 ThinkExist.com Quotations. "Galileo Galilei quotes". ThinkExist.com Quotations Online 1 Oct. 2012. 20 Nov. 2012 <http://en.thinkexist.com/quotes/galileo_galilei/>

It becomes really tempting to reach out to the tree of the knowledge of good and evil and therefore try to use our wisdom to fix what we think is wrong with the world. However, the Bible is warning us that if we focus on solving our problems first and think that afterward we will still have time and energy to keep our garden, we are mistaken. We erroneously think that somehow finding and fixing the cause of our perceived problems will relieve our discomfort. Faith, not wisdom, was given to us to relieve our discomfort. If we can directly take care of a problem, we erroneously think that we are doing a good thing because we are not depleting any of our faith, and we can save our faith for the times when we really need it. We think we are giving faith a break. But just the opposite is true; we won't find true comfort and rest until we turn to faith first and then, having rested in faith, our problems seem to take care of themselves or at least the best solution becomes very clear. I think that is what Vincent van Gogh was getting at when he said,

> It is true that every day has its own evil, and its good too. But how difficult must life be, especially farther on when the evil of each day increases as far as worldly things go, if it is not strengthened and comforted by faith.
>
> —Vincent van Gogh (1853–1890)[36]

We have already learned in Genesis 1 that we cannot exhaust faith or save it up, and we certainly can't give faith a rest; it gives us rest. I can think of countless times when I have forgotten this simple system: I work and faith gives me rest. When I have let my mind run away with things, this has caused me a lot of needless worry.

One example was when my wife and I discovered that our infant son had a rare condition called schizencephaly. We were told that he would most likely develop intractable seizures and not survive infancy. We were devastated to say the least. There was absolutely nothing we could do to undo the problem we had been given. Of course, at that time I had no idea that I had a garden of Eden, let alone that I should first take care of my garden and then take care of my son, or that everything would be fine if I had faith. My attitude was that if I could do just one more thing to help my

36 ThinkExist.com Quotations. "Vincent van Gogh quotes". ThinkExist.com Quotations Online 1 Oct. 2012. 20 Nov. 2012 <http://en.thinkexist.com/quotes/vincent_van_gogh/7.html>

son, then I would have time to rest. But the "one more things" never stopped coming—therapy sessions, doctor's appointments, and oh yes, fun, we had to have fun whether we had any energy or desire for it or not. The rest that I was craving was always put off.

As it turns out, my son is now a junior in college and is currently planning a career in arts management. For me, it turned out to be a great lesson. Since I had been so exhausted trying to fix problems before taking care of faith, this experience taught me undeniably that I needed to always take care of my garden of Eden first. If I had taken care of my tree of life first, then, having rested in faith, I would have been renewed and refreshed so that I could truly be more helpful to my son. I would not only have had more energy to help him, but I would have had better decision-making abilities to know what was and was not important for him. As it was, I was just trying to survive the days.

As I am beginning to understand, I must take care of my garden of Eden, and then I will be of more help to myself and the others around me. I see reminders of this every day. Even when I travel, I am reminded by a steward or stewardess to put my oxygen mask on first before helping others. It makes me smile to think of how many times I have heard that advice and not connected it to the care of my faith. So many things in my life have clearly directed me to take care of my garden of Eden first. Still I wonder why I find it so hard to remember this simple rule all the time and in everything I do.

How many times would I need to make this mistake before I could trust the way the Lord God had set things up? Actually, I should be thankful that I am forgetting this less often and for shorter durations. I certainly need all my wisdom and probably a little more to remember this axiom during the more difficult times.

The point is that our lives will unfold as they will; we should not interpret things as being necessarily good or evil. That will only get us worked up. We should just do our daily business, and if we make it a priority to tend our gardens and know the comfort and rest that faith gives us, we will be at our best and better able to help those around us. If we try to get a better outcome for ourselves by basing everything we do on what we think is good or evil at the time, we will only lose sight of faith. We will be literally chasing good and evil, and true comfort and rest will never be able to find us.

So far Genesis 2 has told us exactly what it takes to have faith in our lives. Trust the way the Lord God has set things up, and find comfort in faith above everything else. The remainder of Genesis 2 gives us an example of how faith and wisdom can work together to our joy and benefit.

> And the LORD God said, It is not good that the man should be alone; I will make him an help meet for him. And out of the ground the LORD God formed every beast of the field, and every fowl of the air; and brought them unto Adam to see what he would call them: and whatsoever Adam called every living creature, that was the name thereof. And Adam gave names to all cattle, and to the fowl of the air, and to every beast of the field; but for Adam there was not found an help meet for him. And the LORD God caused a deep sleep to fall upon Adam, and he slept: and he took one of his ribs, and closed up the flesh instead thereof; And the rib, which the LORD God had taken from man, made he a woman, and brought her unto the man. And Adam said, This is now bone of my bones, and flesh of my flesh: she shall be called Woman, because she was taken out of Man. (Gen. 2:18–23)

What are we supposed to think about this part of the story? At first it sounds a little strange, to say the least. The Lord God no sooner tells Adam that it is not good to be alone than He starts creating animals and bringing them to Adam to name. Were they really looking for a good mate among the animals? Of course not, but it is a good example of how the Lord God wants us to use the two gifts that He has given us. The Bible is telling us that no matter what is "not good" in our lives, if we use our wisdom, our knowledge of good and evil, to be the keeper of our garden of Eden, then everything will work out in the end. Being a good caretaker of a garden means that we need to name the animals that are living in our garden. We need to know who and what they are to keep them and the garden in tip-top shape. In other words, we have to keep abreast of what's going on in our lives that might either enhance or threaten our faith. So in Genesis 2, the creation and naming of animals symbolizes Adam's commitment to caring for the garden. Adam didn't have to use his wisdom to try to solve the problem of not having a mate; he focused on taking care of the garden and all its animals and trusted that a mate would be found in good time.

This does sound a little counterintuitive, but we need to consider the possibilities. The first possibility is that we concentrate on taking care of the garden and trust that a mate will come along. If we get a mate, great, but if for some reason a mate never shows up, we are still in the garden of Eden—not a bad result in either case. The second possibility is that we choose to work on finding a mate at the expense of being the keeper of the garden. If we neglect the garden and don't find a mate either, then we will have nothing. If we fail to care for the garden, we will lose it, whether we find a mate or not. In the next chapter, we will find that things are not so good outside the garden, even with a mate.

That is exactly why the Lord God warned us not to eat of the fruit of the tree of the knowledge of good and evil. The warning is just telling us not to use our knowledge of good and evil—our wisdom—to primarily try to solve our perceived problems before we use it to take care of our own garden of Eden.

Adam naming the animals even though he had no mate is a good example of making the care of his garden a priority. Eventually a mate did come along, and everything worked out. Does this mean we can never use our wisdom and our knowledge of good and evil to try to get something we want? Of course not—as long as our garden is in good order, we can work on anything we want. We should, however, never think that our wisdom could ever give us the comfort and rest that faith does.

> And Adam said, This is now bone of my bones, and flesh of my flesh: she shall be called Woman, because she was taken out of Man. Therefore shall a man leave his father and his mother, and shall cleave unto his wife: and they shall be one flesh. And they were both naked, the man and his wife, and were not ashamed. (Gen. 2:23–25)

Before we conclude the garden of Eden story, there are a few odds and ends that need to be explained. The first is the issue of the four rivers that flow from the garden of Eden. The rivers are a metaphor for the advantages of having faith in our lives. If our garden is well cared for, the rivers will flow out of our garden, out of us, and in all directions to benefit everything and everyone else in our lives. They are like our airplane oxygen masks in that we have to take care of our garden first before helping others, just like we need to put on our own oxygen mask first. As rivers do, they nourish and replenish those who live near them. Likewise with faith, the benefit will be to ourselves and to those around us. We don't have to make the world a better place; we should just be happy with our faith and let it flow from us. In doing so, the world will be a better place. The second verse that needs to be clarified is Genesis 2:24:

> Therefore shall a man leave his father and his mother, and shall cleave unto his wife: and they shall be one flesh.

This too has to be a metaphor since Adam and the woman did not have parents. It implies that when we are children, we learn about faith and derive safety and comfort from our parents' garden of Eden. When we grow up, we must leave this setting, form a new family, and find and be the keeper of our own garden of Eden. With our mate, our gardens merge and become one. We should be aware that if we harm our mate's garden, we harm our own. Likewise, if we neglect our own garden of Eden, we neglect our mate's. Finally we turn to the last verse.

> And they were both naked, the man and his wife, and were not ashamed. (Gen. 2:25)

Adam and his mate were living in their garden of Eden. They were completely at ease with each other. Adam had demonstrated that he knew how to take care of his garden of Eden by naming the animals before he tried to solve his problem of not having a mate. Adam and his mate were living the good life.

In Genesis 1 and 2, the premise for living a good life is clearly presented. Faith is the greatest of all creations; it gives us a profound sense of peace, comfort, and rest. Every human being is given his or her own garden of Eden with two special trees that represent gifts of faith and wisdom. Wisdom's job is to work at keeping this garden healthy and keep both trees growing as they were intended to. If our garden is well cared for, then our wisdom can also see and experience all complexities of a world of good and evil. In this case, wisdom knows that faith will give it peace, comfort, and rest from dealing with this imperfect world.

Now all the components of the story fit into the topic of faith, and Adam and the woman were off to a good start. But there were several questions to be answered. Could Adam continue to be the keeper of the garden? What about the newly formed woman—did she know that she also needed to be the keeper of the garden of Eden, or was it Adam's responsibility to teach her? Did the tree of life have any edible fruit, and if so, what would happen if they ate of it? Can we, in our time, as Adam and the woman did in theirs, live in complete trust of faith the way the Lord God set things up, without challenging the instructions at all? The Bible is not optimistic regarding these questions. Stay tuned for the thrilling action about to take place in "The Garden of Eden, Part II."

> Faith is an act of a finite being who is grasped by, and turned to, the infinite.
>
> —Paul Tillich (1886–1965)[37]

37 ThinkExist.com Quotations. "Paul Tillich quotes". ThinkExist.com Quotations Online 1 Oct. 2012. 20 Nov. 2012 <http://en.thinkexist.com/quotes/paul_tillich/3.html>

CHAPTER 3

The Problem
The Loss of Healthy Faith

Doubt grows with knowledge.
—Johann Wolfgang von Goethe (1749–1832)[38]

GENESIS 3

1 Now the serpent was more subtil than any beast of the field which the LORD God had made. And he said unto the woman, Yea, hath God said, Ye shall not eat of every tree of the garden? 2 And the woman said unto the serpent, We may eat of the fruit of the trees of the garden:

3 But of the fruit of the tree which is in the midst of the garden, God hath said, Ye shall not eat of it, neither shall ye touch it, lest ye die.

---

38 ThinkExist.com Quotations. "Johann Wolfgang von Goethe quotes". ThinkExist.com Quotations Online 1 Oct. 2012. 20 Nov. 2012 <http://en.thinkexist.com/quotes/johann_wolfgang_von_goethe/3.html>

4 And the serpent said unto the woman, Ye shall not surely die:

5 For God doth know that in the day ye eat thereof, then your eyes shall be opened, and ye shall be as gods, knowing good and evil.

6 And when the woman saw that the tree was good for food, and that it was pleasant to the eyes, and a tree to be desired to make one wise, she took of the fruit thereof, and did eat, and gave also unto her husband with her; and he did eat.

7 And the eyes of them both were opened, and they knew that they were naked; and they sewed fig leaves together, and made themselves aprons.

8 And they heard the voice of the LORD God walking in the garden in the cool of the day: and Adam and his wife hid themselves from the presence of the LORD God amongst the trees of the garden.

9 And the LORD God called unto Adam, and said unto him, Where art thou?

10 And he said, I heard thy voice in the garden, and I was afraid, because I was naked; and I hid myself.

11 And he said, Who told thee that thou wast naked? Hast thou eaten of the tree, whereof I commanded thee that thou shouldest not eat?

12 And the man said, The woman whom thou gavest to be with me, she gave me of the tree, and I did eat.

13 And the LORD God said unto the woman, What is this that thou hast done? And the woman said, The serpent beguiled me, and I did eat.

14 And the LORD God said unto the serpent, Because thou hast done this, thou art cursed above all cattle, and above every beast of the field; upon thy belly shalt thou go, and dust shalt thou eat all the days of thy life:

15 And I will put enmity between thee and the woman, and between thy seed and her seed; it shall bruise thy head, and thou shalt bruise his heel.

16 Unto the woman he said, I will greatly multiply thy sorrow and thy conception; in sorrow thou shalt bring forth children; and thy desire shall be to thy husband, and he shall rule over thee.

17 And unto Adam he said, Because thou hast hearkened unto the voice of thy wife, and hast eaten of the tree, of which I commanded thee, saying, Thou shalt not eat of it: cursed is the ground for thy sake; in sorrow shalt thou eat of it all the days of thy life;

18 Thorns also and thistles shall it bring forth to thee; and thou shalt eat the herb of the field;

19 In the sweat of thy face shalt thou eat bread, till thou return unto the ground; for out of it wast thou taken: for dust thou art, and unto dust shalt thou return.

20 And Adam called his wife's name Eve; because she was the mother of all living.

21 Unto Adam also and to his wife did the LORD God make coats of skins, and clothed them.

22 And the LORD God said, Behold, the man is become as one of us, to know good and evil: and now, lest he put forth his hand, and take also of the tree of life, and eat, and live for ever:

> 23 Therefore the LORD God sent him forth from the garden of Eden, to till the ground from whence he was take
>
> 24 So he drove out the man; and he placed at the east of the garden of Eden Cherubims, and a flaming sword which turned every way, to keep the way of the tree of life.

GENESIS 3 INTRODUCES TWO NEW characters, a male serpent and a cherub.39 The story opens with the serpent and closes with the cherub. We will see that each adds to our understanding of faith, and we will start with the serpent. As I have said in the previous chapter, the garden of Eden does not appear to be a perfect place because it has a tree that, if we eat of its fruit, will kill us. Now we see that it has serpents too. Are they good serpents, or are they bad serpents?

It seems to be a popular belief that this serpent in the garden of Eden is the Devil, but I have never been convinced. Whether he is the Devil or not, he is certainly blamed for everything that goes wrong in the story. The woman specifically told the Lord God that the serpent beguiled her into eating the fruit. Was the woman right, or is there another way to interpret this narrative? E. A. Speiser40 has proposed that the way the Hebrew text was written suggests that the woman interrupted the serpent in mid-thought; she didn't let him finish what he wanted to say. If this is true, then the woman did not wait for the serpent to tell her the truth, the whole truth, and nothing but the truth. The woman answered what she thought the serpent's question was by telling him that they should not touch or eat the fruit from the tree in the midst of the garden, lest they die. But the woman's answer did not entirely reflect the Lord God's warning. There were two things that must have concerned the serpent about the woman's answer. First, as far as we know, they were not prohibited from touching the fruit, and second, the woman was ambiguous as to which tree in the midst of the garden from which they should not eat.

---

39 Both cherubim and cherubims seem to be plural for cherub. Whether there is one or more of these creatures at the east of Eden does not seem to matter. I will mainly use the word cherub in this text to indicate the singular and cherubim to indicate the plural.

40 Speiser, E. A. *The Anchor Bible: Genesis*. Garden City, NY: Doubleday, 1964.

The serpent's next move was to try to talk to the woman again, but it is unclear whether she even heard him since she did not acknowledge anything the serpent said. Instead, she started to evaluate the fruit of the tree of the knowledge of good and evil for herself. It seems as though the reasons why the woman ate the fruit of the tree of the knowledge of good and evil were hers and hers alone. The woman was not beguiled by the serpent, though she said she was; she really just seemed to ignore him, and in the end, she even used him as a scapegoat.

With this new understanding, it is certainly possible that the serpent had nothing to do with the reason the woman ate from the tree of the knowledge of good and evil. To illustrate another point of view that might have come from the serpent, I have created a fictional dialogue between Mr. and an assumed Mrs. Serpent.

Mr. Serpent: (As Mr. Serpent remorsefully slithered into his lair on the evening of his falling out with God, he was more than a little anxious. He knew that Mrs. Serpent would not be happy with him.) Honnnney? I have something to tell yooou.

Mrs. Serpent: (Hearing Mr. Serpent's conciliatory voice and having been turned into a snake herself.) What is it that thou hast done now, Mr. Serpent? Hast thou been talking to those humans that I have told thee not to engage thereof, lest we get in trouble with God? The humans are nothing but trouble; they don't listen. And tell me, Mr. Serpent, why am I a snake and no longer a serpent? Just a moment ago I was breathing fire on thy dinner to warm it, and all of a sudden my flame went out and I found myself on the ground with an insatiable hunger for dirt and evil thoughts of wanting to bite the humans. Tell me about that, Mr. Serpent!

Mr. Serpent: Well … it all started when God told me that it was my job to prevent the humans from eating the fruit of the tree of the knowledge of good and evil. He told me that He had made serpents smarter than all the other animals so that we could help the humans. God continued by explaining to me how He had endowed the humans with both faith and the knowledge of good and evil. He planted two trees in the midst of the garden to remind the humans of both gifts. He had given humans the knowledge of good and evil for two reasons. The first reason was so the humans would have an understanding of how to take care of the garden, and the other was so that they could wonder at and experience all the complexities that the world has to offer. The Lord God knew the knowledge of good and evil could quickly overwhelm the humans, so He created faith as a resting place away from seeing all this good and evil. God told me that the knowledge of good and evil was like a roller coaster ride. It was great fun to go for the ride and for even part of the experience to be a little frightened, but if they could never stop the ride and rest, it would soon feel like a punishment. Worse yet, if they could never exit the roller coaster, they would forget that resting was even an option. Without rest, no one could ever enjoy seeing the good and evil in the world, not even God. Without rest, the humans would start believing that all life had to offer was a series of climbs, loops, and drops.

God also told me that was why He gave the humans both faith and the knowledge of good and evil. Faith let them rest after marveling in the experience of seeing good and evil. Likewise, if God hadn't given the humans the capacity to see good and evil, then they wouldn't have needed faith. All that the humans had to do was to make sure they took care of both trees in the garden. The only other thing that the humans could do to mess up the whole thing would be to eat the fruit of the tree of the knowledge of good and evil. If the humans ate from the tree of the knowledge of good and evil, they would be choosing to go on the roller coaster ride for life without faith to comfort them, and as I have said, it can be a pretty scary ride at times. That is why the Lord God told them they would die if they ate of the tree of the knowledge of good and evil; He did not mean that they would literally lose their lives, but they would lose access to the tree of life and the gift of faith. Without faith, they would feel like dying on the roller coaster many times. They would have to scramble for anything that would make them feel better from all the ups and downs of seeing good and evil without faith. So God told me to do whatever it would take to prevent the humans from eating of the tree of the knowledge of good and evil.

Mrs. Serpent: So you went straight to the humans to tell them, right?

Mr. Serpent: Well, yeah! I found the woman first, and I started to reason with her and tried to find out exactly what she already knew. She told me that they were not to eat or touch the fruit of the tree in the midst of the garden, lest they die. At that point I got worried that the woman really didn't understand what God had told her, or maybe that she had gotten the wrong information secondhand from Adam. I should have told her what God told me about why she should not eat of the tree of the knowledge of good and evil, but I didn't get a chance. Instead, because I wanted to make her feel at ease, I started to tell her that God told me that they would not literally die but that their eyes would be made wide open, as if on a roller coaster ride, seeing all the good and evil in the world. If they ate from the tree of the knowledge of good and evil, they would also be like God, but not in a good way. If they ate from the tree of the knowledge of good and evil, they would only be like God in that they would have to create their own system of comfort and rest. God's creation of faith could not help them after they ate. Before I could finish telling the woman everything, she stopped listening to me and started to think to herself and then ... she ate!

Mrs. Serpent: What made you think that you could reason with the humans when God already told them what they shouldn't do? Some things you can't explain to humans. They always think they know better. They hear only what they want to hear and do only what they want to do. Why didn't you just hiss and annoy them every time they reached for the fruit of the tree of the knowledge of good and evil? Sooner or later they would have given up just to avoid the harassment, just as I do when you keep annoying me.

Mr. Serpent: I didn't think of that.

Mrs. Serpent: So then what happened?

Mr. Serpent: The woman handed the fruit to Adam, and he ate it too. Then God came walking through the garden and confronted Adam and the woman, and that is when they blamed me for everything.

Mrs. Serpent: (Being somewhat sarcastic) Why didn't you just run, run to the tree of life for comfort and protection?

Mr. Serpent: (Ignoring the tone in her voice) Because I wanted to explain to God what had happened. But God didn't even let me talk; He just turned me into a snake to crawl on my belly, eat dirt, and bite the humans' heels. For all my effort, I was rewarded with a lifetime of being kicked in the head by the humans and my children and my children's children, etc. I tried to stop them from eating the fruit of the tree of the knowledge of good and evil; but like you said, they don't listen.

Mrs. Serpent: You mean to tell me that you were going to blame the woman for not listening to you right after they both blamed you for everything? That would have sounded real good. But your story does make a lot of sense and certainly explains why I fell to the ground and wanted to eat dirt and bite the humans too. (After a pause of contemplation.) But look on the bright side: the humans are afraid of us, and we don't have to take care of them any longer. (Mr. and Mrs. Serpent engage in an entwining embrace as the lights fade)

Whether this fictional dialogue reflects the true meaning of the story or not does not matter. The story opens the door for reinterpretation. In fact, it is far easier to believe that the story is telling us that humans only listen to what they want to hear and do what they want to do rather than to believe that the serpent represents the actual Devil incarnate. It is clear that the

Bible's point is that every human being, no matter what the cause, winds up eating from the tree of the knowledge of good and evil.

The remainder of Genesis 3 tells us what other things we will experience when we lose access to the comfort of the tree of life. The consequences are presented in two vignettes. The first shows Adam and the woman's initial reaction after eating the fruit of the tree of the knowledge of good and evil. The second takes place with the discussions that the Lord God has with the serpent, the woman, and Adam.

The very first thing Adam and the woman noticed after eating the fruit of the tree of the knowledge of good and evil was their nakedness. They must have been ashamed of their nakedness; otherwise they wouldn't have needed to hide. Compare what Genesis 2 tells us about nakedness with what is found in Genesis 3.

> And they were both naked, the man and his wife, and were not ashamed. (Gen. 2:25)

> And the eyes of them both were opened, and they knew that they were naked; and they sewed fig leaves together, and made themselves aprons. And they heard the voice of the LORD God walking in the garden in the cool of the day: and Adam and his wife hid themselves from the presence of the LORD God amongst the trees of the garden. And the LORD God called unto Adam, and said unto him, Where art thou? And he said, I heard thy voice in the garden, and I was afraid, because I was naked; and I hid myself. And he said, Who told thee that thou wast naked? Hast thou eaten of the tree, whereof I commanded thee that thou shouldest not eat? (Gen. 3:7–11)

So the very first things Adam and the woman felt after eating from the tree of the knowledge of good and evil were shame and fear. Now if something as natural as nakedness is seen in terms of good and evil, then it seems likely that literally everything they saw would have to be characterized as being either good or evil. They would become consumed with classifying things as being either good or evil. Deciding good and evil is also complicated by the fact that some things are good in certain circumstances but not others. I can see why the Lord God told them not to get started with this endless burden of seeing good and evil. The story also tells us that once Adam and the woman defined nakedness as "not good," they felt compelled to do something about it. They sewed fig leaves to cover their nakedness. Instead of faith, they used their own wisdom to try to make them feel better about their nakedness. But would fig leaves make them feel as unashamed as they felt in chapter 2? I don't think so. That is exactly why God created faith in the first place—as a resting place away from this endless task of separating the world up in terms of good and evil. Even God didn't want to get caught in the endless task of assigning good and evil to everything and then adjusting those things according to the circumstances that define whether things are good or evil. God preferred to rest in His creation of faith.

The point is that once we eat from the tree of the knowledge of good and evil, we are obligated to label things as either good or evil, and we forget that we have faith that will separate us from this burden. We forget that our knowledge of good and evil was meant to help us support our faith, our tree of life. After eating from the tree of the knowledge of good and evil, we come to believe that we will find comfort by our own means and that we don't need faith or the tree of life. Thinking about it this way, why would we ever want to eat from the tree of the knowledge of good and evil? The next section of Genesis 3 tells us more about the burden of choosing to eat from the tree of the knowledge of good and evil. The Bible uses the conversations with the serpent, the woman, and Adam to illustrate these consequences.

> And the man said, The woman whom thou gavest to be with me, she gave me of the tree, and I did eat. And the LORD God said unto the woman, What is this that thou hast done? And the woman said, The serpent beguiled me, and I did eat. And the LORD God said unto the serpent, Because thou hast done this, thou art cursed above all cattle, and above every beast of the field; upon thy belly shalt thou go, and dust shalt thou eat all the days of thy life: And I will put enmity between thee and the woman, and between thy

> seed and her seed; it shall bruise thy head, and thou shalt bruise his heel. (Gen. 4:12–15)

I think this part of Genesis 3 can be read just like Genesis 1. But instead of reading it as a poem about the qualities of faith, we can create metaphors for what a life without faith feels like. In this poem we find that the Lord God is not punishing the serpent, the woman, and the man but rather telling them just how bad life will be without faith. As we read the lines, we should think about what they might mean in terms of the absence of faith.

The Lord God addressed the serpent first and turned him into a snake that will forever bite at the humans' heels. The image of snakes biting at our heels brings to my mind the concept of *worry*. Imagine walking in a field on a perfect summer day with not a care in the world until the thought of a snake lying in the weeds enters our minds. That thought would be sure to ruin our walk with worry about what might happen. When we eat of the fruit of the tree of the knowledge of good and evil, we begin to know worry, and once again, faith is not available to comfort us. As a result, now we have shame, fear, and worry in our lives, all from viewing the world only in terms of good and evil. Next, the Lord God turns to the woman.

> Unto the woman he said, I will greatly multiply thy sorrow and thy conception; in sorrow thou shalt bring forth children; and thy desire shall be to thy husband, and he shall rule over thee. (Gen. 3:16)

Here the Bible is not using snakebites but rather the pain of contractions during childbirth to signify that we will experience sorrow as intense as these contractions. This verse is not talking about the actual delivery of an infant as being sorrowful, but rather the events that we face in life, like the death of a loved one, will bring us sorrow as intense as the pains of childbirth. As if living in shame, fear, worry, and now sorrow weren't enough, the Lord God tells us that we will also be ruled by our desires. It tells us that whatever we desire will "control" us. This verse is not just talking about the desire between a woman and a man; any person, place, or thing we desire will rule over us.

This consequence really makes sense to me. If I desire something, it seems to take over my life, and I go out of my way if it means getting closer to the realization of my desire. I would think to myself that once the desire is fulfilled, then it should bring me comfort and joy. But I'll have to admit, once fulfilled, desires rarely give me that much pleasure; I simply move on to the quest of my next desire. I work so hard for the gratification that never comes, the gratification that faith would give me. After eating the fruit of the tree of the knowledge of good and evil, life is not looking too good. Finally the Lord God addresses Adam.

> And unto Adam he said, Because thou hast hearkened unto the voice of thy wife, and hast eaten of the tree, of which I commanded thee, saying, Thou shalt not eat of it: cursed is the ground for thy sake; in sorrow shalt thou eat of it all the days of thy life; Thorns also and thistles shall it bring forth to thee; and thou shalt eat the herb of the field; In the sweat of thy face shalt thou eat bread, till thou return unto the ground; for out of it wast thou taken: for dust thou art, and unto dust shalt thou return. (Gen. 3:17–19)

The curses the Lord God set upon the serpent and the woman certainly apply to Adam too. Everyone will live his or her life in shame, fear, worry, sorrow, and desire. But the Lord God, curiously, does not curse Adam directly. He curses the ground. The ground will produce only thorns and thistles. The Lord God is telling Adam that no matter how hard he tries, he will not be able to grow his own tree of life. Adam will not find happiness, comfort, and rest using his knowledge of good and evil or by his own efforts. True rest and comfort only come from faith. The Lord God did not curse the ground to punish Adam; He did it for Adam's sake, to help him. How so? Well, by telling Adam that he will be wasting his time if he thinks he can create a good life using his own wisdom. Wisdom should be first and foremost the keeper of faith; no human can use his or her wisdom to find true happiness, comfort, or rest. Adam's wisdom cannot help him grow his own tree of life or help him find his way back to the Lord God's tree of life. The Lord God is telling Adam that he can't think his way out of these problems; he'll have to find another way. The following quote captures this idea:

> Faith is an oasis in the heart which can never be reached by the caravan of thinking (wisdom).
>
> —Kahlil Gibran (1883–1931)[41]

The Lord God also tells Adam that without the tree of life in his life, he is only half of what he was meant to be. Adam is only the dust of the ground and will return to the dust again. Without the tree of life, Adam has no faith and is estranged from God. At this point Adam has two choices: he can admit that he cannot use his wisdom to find his way back to the tree of life and ask the Lord God for help, or he can continue to think that eventually his wisdom will solve his problems. The remainder of Genesis 3 completes the story and tells us which of the two options Adam chooses.

> And Adam called his wife's name Eve; because she was the mother of all living. Unto Adam also and to his wife did the LORD God make coats of skins, and clothed them. And the LORD God said, Behold, the man is become as one of us, to know good and evil: and now, lest he put forth his hand, and take also of the tree of life, and eat, and live for ever: Therefore the LORD God sent him forth from the garden of Eden, to till the ground from whence he was taken. (Gen. 3:20–23)

Verses 20 through 23 confirm just how lost Adam was. He had just lost access to the tree of life, and he instantly shifted his attention to his wife. In the story, he did not acknowledge what the Lord God had just told him. Instead he named his wife Eve, which literally means life. Whether Adam knew it or not, he had just turned Eve into his new tree of life, his new desire and source of comfort and rest. The Bible wants us to understand that no thing, person, or place can replace our tree of life. But Adam had decided that Eve, and whatever he found on his own, would bring all the comfort and rest he would need.

---

41 ThinkExist.com Quotations. "Kahlil Gibran quotes". ThinkExist.com Quotations Online 1 Oct. 2012. 20 Nov. 2012 <http://en.thinkexist.com/quotes/kahlil_gibran/4.html>

Since Adam had decided to do without faith, the Lord God needed to make it official. Adam would no longer be the keeper of the garden, and he would not be permitted to eat from the tree of life. Adam would not have the comfort and rest that faith could give him. Adam, at least for the time being, could not live in paradise. Adam had lost a lot. Think about it—what would it be like if we had ready access to the fruit of the tree of life? Any time we felt shame, fear, worry, sorrow, or desire, all we would have to do would be to eat from the tree of life and be refreshed and free of all our shame, fear, worry, sorrow, and desire. This also gets me to think that the so-called forbidden fruit may have been originally from the tree of the knowledge of good and evil, but now for Adam and us too it is from the tree of life.

The story next introduces the second new character, a cherub. The Lord God created the cherub almost as an afterthought to supposedly keep Adam and Eve from getting to the tree of life. Interestingly, the cherub is only mentioned once, in this single verse, in the whole primeval history. This introduction may therefore seem unimportant in the context of the whole story to us, yet if we really stop to think, it is quite profound.

> So he drove out the man; and he placed at the east of the garden of Eden Cherubims, and a flaming sword which turned every way, to keep the way of the tree of life. (Gen. 3:24)

All my life I had interpreted Genesis 3:24 to mean that the Lord God had expelled the humans from the garden of Eden because they had disobeyed Him. The Lord God had placed the cherub—whatever that scary thing was—and a flaming sword to keep the humans out of the garden of Eden forever. But when I thought about it, why didn't the Lord God just destroy the garden? The Lord God didn't need to keep the way of the tree of life for Himself. The Lord God created faith in the beginning and didn't need a tree to remind Him of it. More likely, the Lord God didn't destroy the garden of Eden and the tree of life because He wanted Adam to remember, somewhere in his consciousness, just what the tree of life could do for him.

The message from the Lord God to us is that He wants us to remember that if we really, really want to not feel shame, fear, worry, sorrow, and desire that wisdom brings without faith, all we need to do is follow the way back to the tree of life, knowing that all we need to do is get past the cherub and the flaming sword. We could once again see all the wonders the world had to offer, both good and bad, and also have the comfort and rest of faith. If the Lord God had destroyed the garden or the way to the tree of life, the message would have been clear: we could never find our way back to faith. Since the Lord God left the garden intact in the story, it tells us that faith still exists, even if we think that we don't have ready access to it.

When I think about the image of a path back to the tree of life, with a cherub and a flaming sword, I think how well it describes my feelings about faith. I know faith is there at the end of the path. I can almost see it, but I am so afraid of the cherub and the flaming sword that I think to myself that I would never make it past the guard to reach the tree of life. Being outside the garden, especially when I'm feeling down, I yearn for the tree of life. I alternate between thinking thoughts of, *Why bother? I'll never make it past the cherub,* and *How can I trick the cherub and sneak past him?* I feel trapped in a no-win situation. Would the Bible leave us outside the garden without telling us how to proceed?

As I have discovered, the Bible has been helping me by teaching me what faith is all about. But now the story is telling me that I am excluded from the garden and the tree of life. To get faith back in my life, I will need to challenge a mighty cherub and his flaming sword. How will the Bible help me now? I will just have to be patient and confident that I won't be left hanging. If I just keep reading the Bible, it will certainly tell me what will be required of me to reenter the garden of Eden.

The question arises, then, how must I understand this part of the text to help me with this task? I know that the cherub is the thing that is keeping me from the garden, but what exactly does this ancient figure represent in my life right now? What is keeping me out of the garden today?

Cherubim, according to the *Blue Letter Bible,* represent wisdom[42], so wisdom is keeping us out of the garden of Eden. That is so ironic. I am using my wisdom to try to get back in the garden, and wisdom is not only the thing that got me kicked out of the garden but also is the only thing keeping me out. I'll never be able to use my wisdom to out-trick

42 Blue Letter Bible. "Dictionary and Word Search for keruwh (Strong's 3742)'. Blue Letter Bible. 1996-2012. 21 Nov 2012. <http:// www.blueletterbible.org/lang/lexicon/ lexicon.cfm?Strong's=H3742&t=KJV>

wisdom itself. Wisdom will always know what I'm planning to do. It is like trying to outsmart a mirror. Now I will have to admit, that was a pretty clever move by the Lord. Even if the Lord had placed an army of cherubim with flaming swords before the tree of life, eventually someone from the human race would get through unharmed. Many would fall victim to the flaming sword, but occasionally a human would reenter the garden of Eden. Interestingly, I've never read in the newspaper obituaries any report on the number of deaths caused by cherubim. If only Adam would have realized that it was wisdom keeping him out of the garden, he would have been able to ask the Lord God to help him. The Lord could have told Adam to stop using his wisdom to get past wisdom. Wisdom only knows what your wisdom is about to do and therefore prevents you from crossing, but remember, faith is separate and invisible to wisdom, and through faith we can pass right by the cherubim unseen and unheard.

Adam did not follow this approach because he still thought he knew what was best and that he would figure everything out. With this attitude, it seemed likely that Adam was going to live a life of shame, fear, sorrow, and desire and have no chance of any real comfort.

By the end of Genesis 3, the Lord God's plan had gone awry. Adam had his mate, but he no longer had the comforts of the garden of Eden and the tree of life. This story has given us some very special insights, the most important being that we were given two gifts in the garden of Eden—faith and wisdom—and they were meant to work together. Wisdom works to support faith, and faith comforts wisdom. Being a good keeper of the garden of Eden simply requires that we remember this relationship and hold it above all other endeavors. If we are being good keepers of our gardens, then we will be unashamed like Adam was in chapter 2. If we are not taking good care of our garden, we will feel the pain and suffering of shame, fear, worry, sorrow, and desire. If we experience these feelings in our daily life, it is telling us that there is something wrong with the way we are taking care of our garden of Eden.

With all the suffering that Adam is about to feel outside the garden of Eden, I would be surprised if he wasn't about to raise a little Cain. The next story in the primeval history shows us how the Lord follows Adam out of the garden. The Lord's intentions are not to continue to help Adam but to focus on Cain, Adam's son. Could Cain be convinced that he needed to be the keeper of a garden he had never seen? Would Cain listen to the advice or be like his mother and father, who ignored the Lord God's instructions?

> Faith is not a thing which one "loses," we merely cease to shape our lives by it.
>
> —Georges Bernanos (1888–1948)[43]

43 ThinkExist.com Quotations. "Georges Bernanos quotes". ThinkExist.com Quotations Online 1 Oct. 2012. 20 Nov. 2012 <http://en.thinkexist.com/quotes/georges_bernanos/2.html>

Evil is a personal challenge to every human being
and can be overcome only by faith.
—Immanuel Kant (1724–1804)[44]

Genesis 4

1 And Adam knew Eve his wife; and she conceived, and
bare Cain, and said, I have gotten a man from the LORD. 2
And she again bare his brother Abel. And Abel was a keeper
of sheep, but Cain was a tiller of the ground.

3 And in process of time it came to pass, that Cain brought of the fruit of the ground an offering unto the LORD.

4 And Abel, he also brought of the firstlings of his flock and of the fat thereof. And the LORD had respect unto Abel and to his offering:

5 But unto Cain and to his offering he had not respect. And Cain was very wroth, and his countenance fell.

6 And the LORD said unto Cain, Why art thou wroth? and why is thy countenance fallen?

7 If thou doest well, shalt thou not be accepted? and if thou doest not well, sin lieth at the door. And unto thee shall be his desire, and thou shalt rule over him.

8 And Cain talked with Abel his brother: and it came to pass, when they were in the field, that Cain rose up against Abel his brother, and slew him.

9 And the LORD said unto Cain, Where is Abel thy brother? And he said, I know not: Am I my brother's keeper?

44 See Kant's essay, "Concerning the Possibility of a Theodicy and the Failure of All Previous Philosophical Attempts in the Field" (1791). Stephen Palmquist explains why Kant refuses to solve the problem of evil in "Faith in the Face of Evil", Appendix VI of Kant's Critical Religion (Aldershot: Ashgate, 2000).

10 And he said, What hast thou done? the voice of thy brother's blood crieth unto me from the ground.

11 And now art thou cursed from the earth, which hath opened her mouth to receive thy brother's blood from thy hand;

12 When thou tillest the ground, it shall not henceforth yield unto thee her strength; a fugitive and a vagabond shalt thou be in the earth.

13 And Cain said unto the LORD, My punishment is greater than I can bear.

14 Behold, thou hast driven me out this day from the face of the earth; and from thy face shall I be hid; and I shall be a fugitive and a vagabond in the earth; and it shall come to pass, that every one that findeth me shall slay me.

15 And the LORD said unto him, Therefore whosoever slayeth Cain, vengeance shall be taken on him sevenfold. And the LORD set a mark upon Cain, lest any finding him should kill him.

16 And Cain went out from the presence of the LORD, and dwelt in the land of Nod, on the east of Eden.

17 And Cain knew his wife; and she conceived, and bare Enoch: and he builded a city, and called the name of the city, after the name of his son, Enoch.

18 And unto Enoch was born Irad: and Irad begat Mehujael: and Mehujael begat Methusael: and Methusael begat Lamech.

19 And Lamech took unto him two wives: the name of the one was Adah, and the name of the other Zillah.

20 And Adah bare Jabal: he was the father of such as dwell in tents, and of such as have cattle.

21 And his brother's name was Jubal: he was the father of all such as handle the harp and organ.

22 And Zillah, she also bare Tubalcain, an instructer of every artificer in brass and iron: and the sister of Tubalcain was Naamah.

23 And Lamech said unto his wives, Adah and Zillah, Hear my voice; ye wives of Lamech, hearken unto my speech: for I have slain a man to my wounding, and a young man to my hurt.

24 If Cain shall be avenged sevenfold, truly Lamech seventy and sevenfold.

25 And Adam knew his wife again; and she bare a son, and called his name Seth: For God, said she, hath appointed me another seed instead of Abel, whom Cain slew.

26 And to Seth, to him also there was born a son; and he called his name Enos: then began men to call upon the name of the LORD.

GENESIS 1–3 HAS PRESENTED US with an orderly picture of faith. Genesis 1 told us what faith was like. Genesis 2 told us how to be faith's keeper, and Genesis 3 informed us that it was all too human to reject faith, thinking we can manage our own lives. Genesis 4 is a story that continues to describe this evolving relationship humans have with faith. It begins with the Lord trying to convince Adam's son, Cain, to use his wisdom to become the keeper of the garden of faith (Eden) again and not the keeper of his own garden. Since faith is what we lack when we are outside of the garden of Eden, we can refer to it as our faith garden as opposed to the garden that our wisdom is trying to grow in its attempt to give us peace, comfort, and rest. Wisdom's garden will only produce thorns and thistles, as we have already learned. Genesis 4 then continues with a description of just how bad things can get when Cain doesn't listen and persists in his folly.

To understand the messages found in Genesis 4, we must read it as an autobiography. We find that we have much more in common with Cain than we would ever like to admit. Even though the details may be different, all of our lives are foretold in the story of Cain and his descendants. We all start out like Cain, who above all else intended to please the Lord with his offering, but somehow, beyond our control, we end up estranged from both the Lord and the world. We eventually become as impudent as Lamech, bragging about our prowess and notoriety. We suffer needlessly from shame, fear, worry, sorrow, and desire. Surely what we desire most is a place of rest. The story of Cain and Abel helps us understand how we, trying to live good lives, seem to mess things up so badly. To understand what chapter 4 is telling us about our rift with faith, let's take a closer look at its main characters.

After Adam and Eve were escorted out of the garden of Eden, they had two sons. Their names were Cain and Abel, and they wanted nothing more than to please the Lord. Unfortunately, Cain, the firstling, did not please the Lord at all. On the surface there seems to be no legitimate reason why the Lord did not respect Cain and his offering. To understand why the Lord did what He did in the story, we must use every clue available. One such clue lies in each character's name. As in many literary works, the meaning or sound of a character's name helps us understand the events of the story. Cain's name literally means "smith." This should not be thought of as just a common English family name; instead it implies what we understand the term *blacksmith* to mean. A blacksmith takes iron and forges it into something that is useful to him. Cain therefore represents the force that changes the world to our liking. Putting it another way, Cain represents the force in each of us that tries to change the world into something that fits our wishes. He represents our self-will, our wisdom and our reason. Cain is the personification of the knowledge of good and evil within us.

Knowing what the name *Cain* represents, helps us understand the meaning of Abel's name. Abel means "breath." To understand what breath symbolizes, we need only go back to Genesis 2:

> And the LORD God formed man of the dust of the ground, and breathed into his nostrils the breath of life; and man became a living soul. (Gen. 2:7)

In this verse we find man being formed out of the dust of the ground and the breath of the Lord God. Since the name Abel means "breath," it is easy to conclude that Abel represents the breath of the Lord God, the breath of life. The breath of life certainly aligns itself with the tree of life and the concept of faith, as opposed to the tree of the knowledge of good and evil and the concept of wisdom. Abel represents our life force, our faith.

So now we have the brothers Cain and Abel, instead of the two trees in the garden of Eden, representing wisdom and faith. In fact, since they were a pair of brothers, I don't think it is a stretch to think of the brothers representing the two different sides in every human being. We have our faith side and our wisdom side. If the two brothers represent our faith side and wisdom side, then these parts of us should relate to each other exactly like brothers do, sometimes loving, sometimes fighting, but always coming to the other's assistance in times of need. Some brothers also thrive on rivalry. Even though I don't think Abel had much of a competitive disposition, Cain probably had more than enough drive to win for the both of them. I certainly have felt this brotherly tension in me between my faith side and my wisdom.

When the brothers grew up, Cain decided to bring an offering to the Lord. It appeared that Cain was very confident that he and his offering would be overwhelmingly accepted. If he had been worried about whether he would be accepted, he wouldn't have gotten so angry at his rejection and may have been humble enough to ask the Lord what he could have done to be accepted.

> And in process of time it came to pass, that Cain brought of the fruit of the ground an offering unto the LORD. And Abel, he also brought of the firstlings of his flock and of the fat thereof. And the LORD had respect unto Abel and to his offering: But unto Cain and to his offering he had not respect. And Cain was very wroth, and his countenance fell. (Gen. 4:3–5)

Well, this was an unexpected outcome for Cain, to say the least. Cain had worked hard on his garden. As if to add insult to injury, not only was Cain's offering not respected, but he too was not respected. But why were Cain and his offering rejected while Abel and his offering were accepted? I have never heard a plausible explanation for why the Lord acted as He did.

Cain and Abel's offering to the Lord is one of those points in the Bible that most of us skim over, thinking we don't really need to understand the Lord's rejection of Cain and his offering to understand the whole story. This would be an unfortunate mistake because if we take a little time to wrestle with these verses to find a deeper message, we will be richly rewarded. I feel this is the first of two critical points in the story. If we don't fully understand its message, we will miss the meaning of the entire story. Why was Cain rejected and Abel accepted?

We already know what the names of Cain and Abel mean, but this doesn't explain why the Lord did what He did. Cain represents our wisdom side, and Abel represents our faith side. Since both wisdom and faith were gifts from God, why didn't God accept both sides? We must also use clues from the rest of the primeval history to explain this part of the story. So let's deepen our understanding by comparing both offerers and their offerings in detail.

> Cain, who represents our wisdom side, offered the best from his garden. In Genesis 2, the Lord God had already offered Adam and all of humanity the garden of Eden. The Lord God also told Adam that he would grow only thorns and thistles in his own garden using his own knowledge of good and evil, his own wisdom. Adam could certainly not grow his own tree of life. How could anything Cain grew come close to what was in the garden of Eden? Of course, the Lord God would not respect anything from Cain's garden. The Lord God could not respect Cain either since he was not being the keeper of the garden of Eden; he was trying to be the keeper of his own garden. Was it that Cain didn't know any better? He was a good farmer, and as far as we can tell from the story, he was doing his best. It appears that the fault may lie with his parents. Did they tell him about

the curse the Lord God had placed on the ground? Maybe they were too ashamed to mention it to their children. Cain had also never seen the garden of Eden for himself. Being a farmer, if he had seen the garden of Eden, maybe he would have been so inspired that he would have been more than happy to be its keeper. Regardless of these drawbacks, the Lord could not respect Cain or his offering. The Lord is not interested in what man can accomplish using his own wisdom. The Lord only cares that man uses his wisdom to be the keeper of his garden of Eden.

Nothing in the story gives me the impression that the Lord God was upset or angry with Cain; He was just trying to tell Cain that he was working on the wrong garden. Cain was trying to overcome the curse of the ground by working harder and harder to get the ground to yield a good offering. According to the curse, no matter how hard Cain worked, his garden would never produce a good offering. I'm sure that if Cain would have just asked the Lord, "If working on my garden isn't good enough, then what would You have me work on?" I'm sure that the Lord would have told Cain, "Have I got a garden for you."

Abel, who represents our faith side, offered a firstling. Of course the Lord respects our faith side if we remember that faith is God's highest creation. Abel, being the personification of faith, would naturally be accepted. Abel also knew exactly how the Lord had set things up. The Lord had given us the gift of wisdom to see all the wonders of the world and to be the keeper of our faith. Faith in turn was made to comfort wisdom from all the things it sees and all the work it does. So our faith side, represented by Abel, wanted to rest with the Lord. If faith gives comfort and rest to wisdom, then Abel, our faith side, also wanted to give comfort and rest to Cain, our wisdom side. So how does offering a firstling represent Abel's intentions?

> A firstling refers to the firstborn. The only example of a firstborn we have so far in the Bible is Cain himself. So if Cain represents the wisdom side of a human being, then Abel, by offering a firstling, is offering wisdom back to the Lord God, giving wisdom back to the Lord to do with as the Lord pleases. Of course, the Lord desires for us to use our wisdom to be the keeper of our faith. Additionally, by offering a firstling, Abel (faith) is trying to comfort Cain (wisdom) by suggesting to Cain that all he has to do to be accepted, and more importantly comforted, is to do the Lord's will, not his own. One clear way that we would know that Cain got the message would be to hear Cain tell the Lord that he(wisdom) was not worthy of offering anything to the Lord himself but that he would be happy to take care of his brother (faith). Cain would have been happy to have been his brother's keeper.

Now it is easy to see why Abel and his offering were respected and Cain and his offering were not. The Cain side of us thought it was wise enough to figure out what would please the Lord, but it was so wrong. It didn't even know it was working on the wrong garden. All the Lord God wants our wisdom to do is to be the keeper of our faith, *period*. To help our Cain side realize this, the Lord questioned him. But Cain had already become angry and heartbroken since he had only wanted to please the Lord and had done his best, no matter how misguided. Was Cain in any mood to be open to corrective criticism? The Lord simply asked Cain to tell Him what the problem was.

> And the LORD said unto Cain, Why art thou wroth? and why is thy countenance fallen? If thou doest well, shalt thou not be accepted? and if thou doest not well, sin lieth at the door. And unto thee shall be his desire, and thou shalt rule over him. And Cain talked with Abel his brother. (Gen. 4:6–8)

We find in these verses that Cain was disrespectfully silent. The Lord had asked him a question, and Cain didn't even respond. I'll admit that if I happened to be asked a question directly by the Lord, I'd be speechless too, but I would have certainly been flailing my arms about and trying to speak, pointing to my mouth and indicating that I couldn't possibly talk at all. There is no evidence that Cain even tried to respond to the Lord's question. The Lord, not hearing or seeing any response from Cain, continued by telling him exactly what was going to happen if he continued in his ways. The Lord's warning came in just one simple verse, Genesis 4:7. At first it is hard to understand what this verse is exactly trying to warn us about.

I think that this verse is the second critical point in the story, and once again, if we don't entirely understand all it implies, we will misinterpret the whole story. In fact, I think it is the most misunderstood verse in the whole Bible, and if we misinterpret this verse, we are again at risk for misunderstanding the rest of the Bible's message. Some recent translations of the Bible have compounded the misunderstanding by actually changing the wording from the KJV. Let's compare the KJV to the NLT.

> If thou doest well, shalt thou not be accepted? and if thou doest not well, sin lieth at the door. And unto thee shall be his desire, and thou shalt rule over him. (KJV)

> You will be accepted if you do what is right. But if you refuse to do what is right, then watch out! Sin is crouching at the door, eager to control you. But you must subdue it and be its master. (NLT)

This New Living Translation seems to be saying that we must use our wisdom to subdue, control, and master sin. I think that this is just the opposite of what this verse is really trying to tell us. The Lord does not want us to spend our time subduing sin and being the master of good and evil. He wants us to be free of doing that. The Lord gave us faith so we wouldn't have to wrangle with good and evil all the time. The Lord knows that we are human; we will make many mistakes in our lives. So is this verse in the NLT is telling us that we have to fight off sin all the time? That doesn't sound like anything that the Lord would plan for us. So let's take a closer look at each section of the verse from the King James Version to really find out what the Bible is trying to tell us:

> If thou doest well, shalt thou not be accepted?

If we use our gift of wisdom to be the keeper of our faith, we will be accepted. We will know the profound rest promised to us on the seventh day of creation.

> And if thou doest not well, sin lieth at the door.

If we don't use our wisdom to be faith's keeper, then any sin or mistake we make will cause us needless shame, fear, worry, sorrow, and desire. By not being the keeper of faith, we cannot expect faith to comfort us.

> And unto thee shall be his desire, and thou shalt rule over him.

Shame, fear, worry, sorrow, and desire will cause great angst in our lives and demand our attention. They will not leave us alone until we address them and resolve their demands. They will burden us, and we will want relief from these burdens. We will have to decide how to manage and control them ourselves since we do not have faith to take care of them. We become the ruler over our sins, whether we like it or not. We are in charge of relieving our shame, fear, worry, and desire that develop from these sins. Faith, not wisdom, was created to relieve our shame, fear, worry, sorrow, and desire. The Lord created faith so we will not be burdened by shame, fear, worry, sorrow, and desire; but we must be faith's keeper for this to work.

The Lord was trying to help Cain to figure out just how to be the keeper of his faith's garden and not just his wisdom's garden. The message to us, the readers, is that not only is our wisdom not wise enough to know what to offer the Lord, but it is also not even wise enough to answer the Lord when He directly asks us a question. Instead of engaging the Lord, Cain talked to his brother. About what they spoke is not revealed in the story, but it probably didn't go well since the next thing we hear about is that Cain rose up against Abel and in the end killed him.

> And Cain talked with Abel his brother: and it came to pass, when they were in the field, that Cain rose up against Abel his brother, and slew him. (Gen. 4:8)

So what has just happened? Cain had just killed Abel; our wisdom side had just killed our faith side. This event seems to answer one of the unresolved questions from Genesis 2 and 3. That is, why didn't Adam and the woman die after they ate from the tree of the knowledge of good and evil?

> But of the tree of the knowledge of good and evil, thou shalt not eat of it: for in the day that thou eatest thereof thou shalt surely die. (Gen. 2:17)

The answer is simply that if we eat of the tree of the knowledge of good and evil, we won't physically die, but the faith side of us will die at the hands of the wisdom side of us.

The Lord did not give up on Cain yet. The Lord engaged Cain a second time by asking him another question.

> And the LORD said unto Cain, Where is Abel thy brother? And he said, I know not: Am I my brother's keeper? And he said, What hast thou done? the voice of thy brother's blood crieth unto me from the ground. And now art thou cursed from the earth, which hath opened her mouth to receive thy brother's blood from thy hand; When thou tillest the ground, it shall not henceforth yield unto thee her strength; a fugitive and a vagabond shalt thou be in the earth. (Gen. 4:9–12)

At least Cain was talking to the Lord, but I'm afraid it wasn't in a productive fashion. Knowing that Abel represents our faith side, Genesis 4:9 can be translated as:

> And the LORD said unto Cain, Where is your faith? And he said, I know not: Am I my faith's keeper?

By this time the Lord had obviously had it with Cain since he had no comprehension of the fact that he was supposed to be the keeper of his faith. He was supposed to act like faith's big brother, but that was far from what had just happened. The Lord simply did not want to hear another word and went into a monologue to inform Cain what was going to happen next. Cain would become a fugitive and be filled with shame, fear, worry, sorrow, and desire. He would be alienated from the earth and the heavens. He would not know peace, rest, or comfort. But then the Lord did something unexpected after Cain complained that he could not endure his condition.

And Cain said unto the LORD, My punishment is greater than I can bear. Behold, thou hast driven me out this day from the face of the earth; and from thy face shall I be hid; and I shall be a fugitive and a vagabond in the earth; and it shall come to pass, that every one that findeth me shall slay me. And the LORD said unto him, Therefore whosoever slayeth Cain, vengeance shall be taken on him sevenfold. And the LORD set a mark upon Cain, lest any finding him should kill him. And Cain went out from the presence of the LORD, and dwelt in the land of Nod, on the east of Eden. (Gen. 4:13–16)

In these verses we find Cain using his wisdom to try to negotiate a better deal for himself with the Lord. Was Cain looking for a full pardon? That is unlikely, but what the Lord says to Cain in response seems equally unlikely. The Lord tells Cain that whoever avenges the murder of Abel will be avenged seven times. Whether we believe Cain deserved to be killed for his brother's murder or not, the Bible is informing us that no one should judge Cain. Everyone loses their faith just like Cain, and we should identify with him, not judge him.

The sad fact is that even now when we read Genesis 4, we judge Cain rather than identifying with him. When we judge Cain, we become seven times the vagabond and fugitive that Cain was. Instead, we should recognize that we are just like Cain; we are all vagabonds and fugitives. With this, the Bible is trying to tell us that recognizing our situation is the first step to finding our way back to the garden of Eden.

We just learned in Genesis 3 that using our own wisdom as we see fit gets and keeps us out of the garden of Eden. If we turn around and use that wisdom to also judge others, we are just getting farther and farther away from the garden of Eden and our own faith. Cain himself seems to be pretty far from the garden of Eden, and we get the idea that it will take some time for him to find his way back, if he does at all. As Cain leaves the Lord to dwell east of Eden, we wonder just what kind of life a vagabond and fugitive will have.

> And Cain knew his wife; and she conceived, and bare Enoch: and he builded a city, and called the name of the city, after the name of his son, Enoch. And unto Enoch was born Irad: and Irad begat Mehujael: and Mehujael begat Methusael: and Methusael begat Lamech. And Lamech took unto him two wives: the name of the one was Adah, and the name of the other Zillah. And Adah bare Jabal: he was the father of such as dwell in tents, and of such as have cattle. And his brother's name was Jubal: he was the father of all such as handle the harp and organ. And Zillah, she also bare Tubalcain, an instructer of every artificer in brass and iron: and the sister of Tubalcain was Naamah. And Lamech said unto his wives, Adah and Zillah, Hear my voice; ye wives of Lamech, hearken unto my speech: for I have slain a man to my wounding, and a young man to my hurt. If Cain shall be avenged sevenfold, truly Lamech seventy and sevenfold. (Gen. 4:17–24)

The second part of Genesis 4 is, in a lot of respects, easier to understand than the first part. For all practical purposes, Cain does not appear to be a fugitive or a vagabond, at least in our sense of what these terms ordinarily mean. Cain seems to be doing very normal things, like taking a wife, having children, and building things. The story talks about very familiar human accomplishments like making music and forging brass, rather than things that are beyond our everyday experience, like conversing with the Lord and suffering heavenly curses. I think the Bible is making the point that we see the world just like Cain and his descendants saw the world, and we do things just like Cain and his descendants did things. We have all allowed our wisdom to create and accomplish many things, but we have not let it be the keeper of our faith. In fact, we need to realize the normal things that Cain did—the things we do in our normal lives—are things that prevented him and prohibit us from being the keepers our own faith garden. We have used these normal things of daily life to distract us. We still think that if we try hard enough, using our own wisdom, we will eventually find the peace, comfort, and rest that we are searching for, the rest that faith would give us.

After many generations, we come to Lamech. Lamech's offenses against others have multiplied those of Cain's. Lamech had misused his wisdom for so many things of his own choosing that he would probably never be able to change and become the keeper of his faith's garden. Lamech's will be done, not the Lord's. Lamech is so far down the wrong path he doesn't even know what he doesn't know. The question the Bible poses to us with this part of the story is whether we have to deteriorate as much as Lamech did to realize that asserting our wisdom on the world will only compound our shame, fear, worry, sorrow, and desire. If we are trying to find happiness, comfort, and rest, then wisdom is not only a dead-end road, but it is deadly for those around us as well. The Bible then returns to Adam and Eve and a replacement for the slain Abel.

> And Adam knew his wife again; and she bare a son, and called his name Seth: For God, said she, hath appointed me another seed instead of Abel, whom Cain slew. And to Seth, to him also there was born a son; and he called his name Enos: then began men to call upon the name of the LORD. (Gen. 4:25–26)

The Bible has left Cain's descendants hopelessly lost, but would the Lord hear the calls of Seth's descendants? Would He answer, or was He through helping man to see that he must be the keeper of his faith? The next chapter tells us that the Lord gives us at least some compensation for the mess that our wisdom side has gotten us into.

> No man chooses evil because it is evil; he only mistakes it for happiness, the good he seeks.
>
> —Mary Wollstonecraft Shelley (1759–1797)[45]

45 ThinkExist.com Quotations. "Mary Wollstonecraft Shelley quotes". ThinkExist.com Quotations Online 1 Oct. 2012. 20 Nov. 2012 <http://en.thinkexist.com/quotes/mary_wollstonecraft_shelley/>

The disease with which the human mind now labors is want of faith.
—Ralph Waldo Emerson (1803–1882)[46]

Genesis 5

1 This is the book of the generations of Adam. In the day that God created man, in the likeness of God made he him;2 Male and female created he them; and blessed them, and called their name Adam, in the day when they were created.

3 And Adam lived an hundred and thirty years, and begat a son in his own likeness, after his image; and called his name Seth:

4 And the days of Adam after he had begotten Seth were eight hundred years: and he begat sons and daughters:

5 And all the days that Adam lived were nine hundred and thirty years: and he died.

6 And Seth lived an hundred and five years, and begat Enos:

7 And Seth lived after he begat Enos eight hundred and seven years, and begat sons and daughters:

8 And all the days of Seth were nine hundred and twelve years: and he died.

9 And Enos lived ninety years, and begat Cainan:

10 And Enos lived after he begat Cainan eight hundred and fifteen years, and begat sons and daughters:

46 ThinkExist.com Quotations. "Ralph Waldo Emerson quotes". ThinkExist.com Quotations Online 1 Oct. 2012. 20 Nov. 2012 <http://en.thinkexist.com/quotes/ralph_waldo_emerson/42.html>

11 And all the days of Enos were nine hundred and five years: and he died.

12 And Cainan lived seventy years, and begat Mahalaleel:

13 And Cainan lived after he begat Mahalaleel eight hundred and forty years, and begat sons and daughters:

14 And all the days of Cainan were nine hundred and ten years: and he died.

15 And Mahalaleel lived sixty and five years, and begat Jared:

16 And Mahalaleel lived after he begat Jared eight hundred and thirty years, and begat sons and daughters:

17 And all the days of Mahalaleel were eight hundred ninety and five years: and he died.

18 And Jared lived an hundred sixty and two years, and he begat Enoch:

19 And Jared lived after he begat Enoch eight hundred years, and begat sons and daughters:

20 And all the days of Jared were nine hundred sixty and two years: and he died.

21 And Enoch lived sixty and five years, and begat Methuselah:

22 And Enoch walked with God after he begat Methuselah three hundred years, and begat sons and daughters:

23 And all the days of Enoch were three hundred sixty and five years:

24 And Enoch walked with God: and he was not; for God took him.

25 And Methuselah lived an hundred eighty and seven years, and begat Lamech:

26 And Methuselah lived after he begat Lamech seven hundred eighty and two years, and begat sons and daughters:

27 And all the days of Methuselah were nine hundred sixty and nine years: and he died.

28 And Lamech lived an hundred eighty and two years, and begat a son:

29 And he called his name Noah, saying, This same shall comfort us concerning our work and toil of our hands, because of the ground which the LORD hath cursed.

30 And Lamech lived after he begat Noah five hundred ninety and five years, and begat sons and daughters:

31 And all the days of Lamech were seven hundred seventy and seven years: and he died.

32 And Noah was five hundred years old: and Noah begat Shem, Ham, and Japheth.

MY COUNTENANCE CERTAINLY HAD FALLEN after reading the story of Cain and his descendants; was all of humanity fated to become and stay just like Lamech? Genesis 5 tells us that the Lord gives us some compensation for the faith we have lost. To appreciate the message Genesis 5 gives us about faith, we need to review the events of the primeval history once again.

Genesis 1 starts with the creation of faith, the most wonderful thing in the universe. Genesis 2 tells us that we as humans were given the gift of faith along with the gift of wisdom. The gift of wisdom allowed us to be the keeper of our faith and to see all the wonders life had to offer, both good and evil. Faith was given to us so we would not be tormented by seeing all the good and evil. Instead we could find rest in a place removed from all the good and evil. In Genesis 3 we find that humans decide that they really didn't think they needed what faith had to offer them. Genesis 4 followed by telling us that humans discovered that they can use their wisdom to do many things, like build cities, play music, and forge tools. As they became occupied with the things they could do with their wisdom, they became more distant to faith than ever before. They had become fugitives from faith. By the end of Genesis 4, the Lord had given up on Cain's descendants and started to focus on a replacement for the slain Abel, Seth. The end of Genesis 4 transitions us from the problem to the solution of this lack of faith.

> And Adam knew his wife again; and she bare a son, and called his name Seth: For God, said she, hath appointed me another seed instead of Abel, whom Cain slew. And to Seth, to him also there was born a son; and he called his name Enos: then began men to call upon the name of the LORD. (Gen. 4:25–26)

From a literary perspective, the Bible has already used its verses to connect the primeval history stories together, and Genesis 4 and 5 are no different. For example, the Bible uses day seven of creation to be both the conclusion to Genesis 1 and the introduction to Genesis 2. In the same fashion, the final verses of Genesis 4 concluded chapter 4 and introduced us to what will happen in chapter 5. The final verses in Genesis 4 tell us that Seth was Abel's replacement, and therefore, he will represent faith, just as Abel did. This replacing of Abel is also demonstrated in the meaning of Seth's name. Seth means "compensation." He is compensation to Adam and Eve for their murdered son, and for us it is compensation for the loss of faith we all suffer when our Cain side kills our Abel side. The Bible is telling us that even though we may think our faith is dead, the Lord has already planned to compensate us for this.

Genesis 4 also tells us that men began to call upon the name of the Lord. Calling upon the name of the Lord certainly implies that Seth's descendants had a longing to have faith in their lives once again. They wanted to be the keepers of faith but did not know how to do it. Calling on the Lord was a good start, but the important question was, would the Lord respond since

He had had such bad luck in dealing with Cain's side of the family? Now let's turn to reading Genesis 5 as the beginning of a prescription to reinvigorate our faith, to raise the Abel side of us.

> This is the book of the generations of Adam. In the day that God created man, in the likeness of God made he him; Male and female created he them; and blessed them, and called their name Adam, in the day when they were created. And Adam lived an hundred and thirty years, and begat a son in his own likeness, after his image; and called his name Seth. (Gen. 5:1–3)

When we start reading Genesis 5, we immediately think of it as being very familiar but certainly not continuing with the story line of Genesis 4 at all. Genesis 5 takes us right back to day six of the creation poem and the creation of humans.

> So God created man in his own image, in the image of God created he him; male and female created he them. And God blessed them, and God said unto them, Be fruitful, and multiply, and replenish the earth, and subdue it: and have dominion over the fish of the sea, and over the fowl of the air, and over every living thing that moveth upon the earth. (Gen. 1:27–28)

Since Genesis 5 takes us back to the creation poem found in Genesis 1, it is logical to read Genesis 5 as a poem too. We can read it as another poem about faith, but Genesis 5 has a very different message. I think the main message found in this new poem about faith is about how faith survives even when our Cain side tries to murder our Abel side. It seems logical that we cannot really kill the faith in us because it is a gift from the Lord God, but we can certainly ignore the gift. So no matter how hard we try to extinguish faith, it will still reside in us. This is certainly a comforting thought, but just how faint has our faith become? How long will it take before it will reappear? Will it ever be strong enough to comfort us and give us rest from all the shame, fear, worry, sorrow, and desire we feel in our lives? Let's see what this poem is telling us about how long it will take to get faith back first. How long will it take to raise the Abel side of us?

In Genesis 1 God completed and rested in His creation of faith in seven days. In Genesis 5, it takes seven generations for Enoch to walk with God. The story is telling us that it takes a very long time to find our faith. Now I don't think that the Bible is telling us that it literally takes seven generations for one person to rekindle his faith, although that would be a good argument for reincarnation. It is just telling us that it takes a lot longer to get faith back than it did to receive it in the first place.

Even though Genesis 5 seems to be one of those chapters we would like to skip over because there does not seem to be any action taking place, it is an excellent reminder of just how helpless we are in rediscovering our faith. As for the lack of action, that reminds me of just how long I tried to figure faith out using my own wisdom, chasing this theory or that guru. It wasn't till I was in my forties that I decided to give up the chase and sit down alone with the Bible my mother had gotten for me that one Christmas when my faith started appearing. While reading that Bible, my conscious brain, my wisdom, started to quiet, and my faith started emerging even though I was not consciously aware of it happening. Just like in Genesis 5, nothing is happening on the surface, but faith is continuing like a thread through the generations. It was a thread from Adam to Noah that had at least the hope for faith in it. The family line of hope goes from Adam to Seth, to Enos, to Cainan, to Mahalaleel, to Jared, to Enoch, to Methuselah, to Lamech, and to Noah. While reading the chapter, I thought the Bible was going out of its way to tell us that this thread of faith is passed on through the generation in ordinary men. They were not the fathers of anything like cities, cattle ranching, music, or metallurgy, as we had found with the descendants of Cain. They were not even priests as far as the Bible tells us, but they were the figures that kept the hope for faith alive while Cain and his descendants tried to find their own way in life. Genesis 5 gives us hope that there is a way to have faith back in our lives.

Genesis 5 once again is telling us that faith is not something wisdom can figure out. We cannot raise our Abel side from the dead by using our conscious efforts; we need help. Seth's descendants certainly called upon the name of the Lord for this help. We also learned that just calling upon the

Lord for help will take a very long time to rediscover faith. The final verses of Genesis 5 tell us that someone may be able to help us find faith in a more timely way.

> And Lamech lived an hundred eighty and two years, and begat a son: And he called his name Noah, saying, This same shall comfort us concerning our work and toil of our hands, because of the ground which the LORD hath cursed. And Lamech lived after he begat Noah five hundred ninety and five years, and begat sons and daughters: And all the days of Lamech were seven hundred seventy and seven years: and he died. And Noah was five hundred years old: and Noah begat Shem, Ham, and Japheth. (Gen. 5:28–32)

Before we get to Noah, isn't it interesting that a Lamech is the father of Noah and a different Lamech is the descendent of Cain and represents our wisdom at its worst? I believe this fact is just meant to remind us that soon our two forces that had split apart, faith and wisdom, will be in harmony if we follow Noah's lead. The reason Noah will tell us what to do to get our faith back comes from his father's description of him and the meaning of the name Noah.

Genesis 5:29 tells us directly that Noah will comfort us from the curse that the Lord had placed on the ground. Noah will tell us how to become the keeper of the garden of Eden and our faith again. Not surprisingly, the name Noah means "rest." I can only assume that this means the kind of rest we read about on the seventh day of creation with God. Noah will show us how to rest.

By the end of chapter 5, we have a clear picture as to what the problem was that we all faced. We had decided, along with Adam and Eve, that we didn't need faith to comfort us; that we could find enough peace and rest with our own wisdom to get by. In Genesis 4 we found out that this was not true. All that wisdom alone gave us were more thorns and thistles. We were in a bad spot, so in Genesis 5 we cried out for help to the Lord God. The Lord God answered in two ways; first He demonstrated that faith is re-achievable through Enoch and second that Noah would instruct us on how exactly to re-achieve faith.

There are two kinds of people one can call reasonable: those who serve God with all their heart because they know him, and those who seek him with all their heart because they do not know him.

—Blaise Pascal (1623–1662)[47]

47 Blaise Pascal. BrainyQuote.com, Xplore Inc, 2012. http://www.brainyquote.com/quotes/quotes/b/blaisepasc402230.html, accessed November 21, 2012.

Chapter 4

The Prescription
The Restoration of Healthy Faith

Be careful, lest in casting out your demon you exorcise the best thing in you.
—Friedrich Nietzsche (1844–1900)[48]

Introduction to the Noah Story

When I started reading Genesis, beginning at chapter 1 with the days of creation as metaphors for faith, it was at first very difficult because I kept finding myself unconsciously switching back to reading it as the creation of the physical world. By the end of Genesis 5, I had become very comfortable seeing the metaphors in the stories. I could readily apply the stories to my life and did not get distracted by the literal details. Something changed when I started the Noah story. My ability to see the metaphors in the story fell apart. I again found myself reading the account of Noah as a

48 CosmicQuotes.com. "Friedrich Nietzsche quotes". CosmicQuotes.com quotations online 1 Oct. 2012. 20 Nov. http://www.cosmicquotes.com/quotes/authors/f/friedrich_nietzsche/friedrich_nietzsche_7.html

literal story about a flood that had happened thousands of years ago, and I missed the points it had to tell me about faith. I think this occurred because the story was both comfortingly familiar to me and horrifically cruel to its characters. I could not reconcile these two impressions. Let me explain a little more.

Right from our births, the Noah story influences our lives. What infant's world doesn't have at least one reference to Noah, be it on wallpaper or mobiles? Noah, the ark, or its animals can also be found appliquéd on bottles, bowls, and blankets. It is not surprising that children think of Noah as a kind, heroic man who saved the animals. If we continue to be influenced by the story in our teen years, we focus on the carnage that takes place when all of humanity, except one family, was killed in a particularly terrifying way. We sympathetically identify with the drowning victims, not Noah. We question why Noah happened to be the only one saved. Weren't there any other people who were just? Think of the children. How many innocent children struggled in the flood water until, one by one, they took their last breaths? Wasn't Noah just a selfish old man looking out for himself and his family? That is where I left the story so many years ago and where I picked it up again when I received my Christmas present Bible.

So how could I get over these interpretations and focus on what the story had to tell me about faith? I found three ways to pry my mind out of a literal interpretation. The first was to see Noah not as a tainted hero who had saved the animals and watched all humanity drown, but instead to see Noah as representing every man or every woman. All of us have been given a chance to start over in our faith; not just Noah. I decided to identify with Noah even if I didn't know why I should. It was, in itself, a leap of faith for me.

The second reorientation I made was to interpret the story with the information I had already gotten from the metaphors I learned in Genesis 1 through 5. One example of using other stories to understand the Flood story is to see what Noah's name means in terms of the story of faith. Noah means "rest" in Hebrew. The only other reference to the concept of rest comes from God resting on the seventh day of creation, in Genesis 2. Therefore, Noah will show us how to rest with God, which, as stated before, is the ultimate metaphor for faith. Without the earlier chapters, we would not know this.

Finally, the third way I found to see the metaphor in the story was to think to myself that if the Bible wanted us to literally construct an ark to restore our faith, then I'm sure many devout entrepreneurs throughout the ages would have developed big box stores called Arks 'R Us, Ark-Mart, and Ark Depot. Then we would have ready access to ark-building supplies. Okay, so I'm taking things to the absurd again. My point is that I needed to stop reading the story so grimly and read the story seeing that Noah really does solve the problem of the curse on the ground, and I better start trying to understand it for my own benefit.

Before we begin reading the Noah story, it is good to know that it is organized into three chapters. The three chapters in turn talk about how we need to confront events in our past, our present, and our future as they relate to faith. So let's begin reading Genesis 6 and see what it has to tell us about dealing with our past and how it will help us rediscover faith.

> Faith is not belief without proof, but trust without reservation.
>
> —D. Elton Trueblood (1900–1994)[49]

49 D. Elton Trueblood. BrainyQuote.com, Xplore Inc, 2012. http://www.brainyquote.com/quotes/quotes/d/deltontru130096.html, accessed November 21, 2012.

A living faith cannot be manufactured by the rule of the majority.
—Mahatma Gandhi (1869–1948)[50]

Genesis 6

1 And it came to pass, when men began to multiply on the
face of the earth, and daughters were born unto them, 2 That
the sons of God saw the daughters of men that they were
fair; and they took them wives of all which they chose.

3 And the LORD said, My spirit shall not always strive with man, for that he also is flesh: yet his days shall be an hundred and twenty years.

4 There were giants in the earth in those days; and also after that, when the sons of God came in unto the daughters of men, and they bare children to them, the same became mighty men which were of old, men of renown.

5 And God saw that the wickedness of man was great in the earth, and that every imagination of the thoughts of his heart was only evil continually.

6 And it repented the LORD that he had made man on the earth, and it grieved him at his heart.

7 And the LORD said, I will destroy man whom I have created from the face of the earth; both man, and beast, and the creeping thing, and the fowls of the air; for it repenteth me that I have made them.

8 But Noah found grace in the eyes of the LORD.

50 ThinkExist.com Quotations. "Mahatma Gandhi quotes". ThinkExist.com Quotations Online 1 Oct. 2012. 21 Nov. 2012 <http://en.thinkexist.com/quotes/mahatma_gandhi/15.html>

9 These are the generations of Noah: Noah was a just man and perfect in his generations, and Noah walked with God.

10 And Noah begat three sons, Shem, Ham, and Japheth.

11 The earth also was corrupt before God, and the earth was filled with violence.

12 And God looked upon the earth, and, behold, it was corrupt; for all flesh had corrupted his way upon the earth.

13 And God said unto Noah, The end of all flesh is come before me; for the earth is filled with violence through them; and, behold, I will destroy them with the earth.

14 Make thee an ark of gopher wood; rooms shalt thou make in the ark, and shalt pitch it within and without with pitch.

15 And this is the fashion which thou shalt make it of: The length of the ark shall be three hundred cubits, the breadth of it fifty cubits, and the height of it thirty cubits.

16 A window shalt thou make to the ark, and in a cubit shalt thou finish it above; and the door of the ark shalt thou set in the side thereof; with lower, second, and third stories shalt thou make it.

17 And, behold, I, even I, do bring a flood of waters upon the earth, to destroy all flesh, wherein is the breath of life, from under heaven; and every thing that is in the earth shall die.

18 But with thee will I establish my covenant; and thou shalt come into the ark, thou, and thy sons, and thy wife, and thy sons' wives with thee.

19 And of every living thing of all flesh, two of every sort shalt thou bring into the ark, to keep them alive with thee; they shall be male and female.

20 Of fowls after their kind, and of cattle after their kind, of every creeping thing of the earth after his kind, two of every sort shall come unto thee, to keep them alive.

21 And take thou unto thee of all food that is eaten, and thou shalt gather it to thee; and it shall be for food for thee, and for them.

22 Thus did Noah; according to all that God commanded him, so did he.

Building an Ark out of Our Past

As I have stated in the introduction to the Noah story, Genesis 6 was difficult for me to read at first. As we start the Noah story, it seems to have a completely different account of the beginning of time. It is not at all like the beginning we have learned about in Genesis 2. At first we have no idea about what these verses are talking; there were no sons of God, lands of giants, or men of renown in the previous chapters. The people of Noah's generation did not seem to know about the lives of Adam and Eve in the garden of Eden.

What is the Bible trying to tell us? I think the simplest understanding of these verses leads us to believe that the people of Noah's generation did not know exactly what the past was like. Since they did not seem to know about Adam before he left the garden, they had no idea what living with faith was like and why the Lord God had cursed the ground. Their image of the past had become speculative and involved giants and men of renown. Instead of remembering that their ancestors lived in the garden of Eden, they believed that there were marriages between heavenly and earthly beings.

Noah's generation knew one thing, though—that somehow and for some reason things had gone terribly wrong, so much so that the Lord God felt it was necessary to curse the ground for man's sake. But even if Noah's generation didn't know why, we know why God cursed the ground. Adam had decided to reject God's plan and to search for his own happiness, peace, and rest. We also know that Adam's descendants then multiplied the problem and became progressively more unfaithful. By the time Noah was born, God was on the brink of destroying everything He had created. It seems as though even God had lost faith in faith and was ready to give it up with the rest of creation.

This feeling of losing faith in faith was what I experienced before the stories in Genesis started talking to me in the language of metaphor. In my late thirties, before I received that Bible for Christmas from my mother, I knew that faith was supposed to be a part of me, but something had gone wrong before I even knew that something could go wrong. I was at a loss to trace my footsteps back to a time when I was filled with faith. This longing for faith was in me because I knew that at some point in my life I had been filled with faith, and I missed having it. I desperately wanted to re-experience the faith I had been given from the beginning. I wanted to go home—my faith home.

Was going back even an option? I thought not. Worse yet, I had no idea how to move forward to get more faith in my life. I was stuck, not able to go either direction. It seemed that the harder I tried to use my wisdom to get closer to faith, the further away faith became. Every thought I had was only giving me thorns and thistles. I was in a very disparaging place. I was unhappy with my life, and I was at a point of giving up on faith and life itself. At that time, I made a serious attempt at suicide. The details aren't important, but I did spend some time in an ICU and later in a locked psychiatric ward. For years I carried the guilt of that act with me, and I felt shame, fear, worry, and sorrow and even some unrealistic desire to go back and undo everything I had done. Little did I know at the time that my suicide incident would be the key to helping me understand the Noah story and my path back to faith.

Let's turn back to the story and see how Noah will help us to "un-curse" the ground and get back to faith. As I have said, Genesis 6 was hard to read at first. On the other hand, it was easy to see that Genesis 6 was mainly a set of instructions on building an ark. But how could I translate Noah's instructions on building a literal ark into something I could use to help me build or discover the way back to faith? What was the story telling me to build in my life? Before we can understand how these instructions show us how to find faith, let's review what the previous stories have told us about faith, wisdom, and the curse:

> Genesis 1–2:4a tells us that resting with God on the seventh day of creation is the ultimate metaphor for faith.
>
> Genesis 2 tells us that we are the keepers of faith. We use our wisdom to be, above all else, the keepers of faith. We are warned not to solve problems like not having a mate before we make sure our faith is in good order. The symbol for being a good keeper of our faith is being a good keeper of the animals in our garden. This should not be taken literally. It is just meant to show that we know what's in our garden and what is needed to keep everything working together.

> From Genesis 3, we find out that the curse was placed on the ground for man's sake. Adam (man) had decided to use his wisdom as he saw fit and to follow his own wisdom to find happiness, peace, and rest. He thought he did not need to be the keeper of faith. By cursing the ground, the Lord God was telling Adam that his wisdom would only produce thorns and thistles, not happiness, peace, and rest. Rather than rest, the thorns and thistles Adam grew would cause him feelings of shame, fear, worry, sorrow, and desire. The Lord God then sent Adam from the garden of Eden to try to find his own happiness. A cherub with a flaming sword prevented Adam's return into the garden of Eden. But we find out that the cherub represents Adam's own wisdom. Adam is both led out and banned from the garden by his own wisdom.
>
> Genesis 4 tells us about Cain and shows us just how far we can follow our wisdom, looking for happiness, peace, and rest.
>
> In Genesis 5, Noah's father tells us that Noah will comfort us from the Lord's curse. Noah will show us the way back to faith. We also know that in Hebrew, Noah's name means "rest." In other words, Noah will teach us how to undo the curse and find true rest, as described on the seventh day of creation.

Genesis 1–5 has told us that only faith will give us true rest and that our wisdom is the only thing that is preventing us from returning to faith. So how does Genesis 6 instruct us in getting faith back in our lives? Since our own wisdom is what is getting in our way of seeing faith, then it would make sense that Noah would show us how to stop using our wisdom so that we too can see faith. The Noah story will explain how building an ark will stop us from using our wisdom to find happiness, peace, and rest.

For the modern ear, this is a very curious answer. I have never heard any religion propose building an ark to regain faith. I naturally assumed that to find faith, the answer would be more reasonable. For example, go to church and sing songs, give thanks to the Lord in prayer and meditation or do good deeds, and follow the Ten Commandments. Instead of doing all this to find faith, are we supposed to go looking for a gopher tree, since we are told that Noah's ark was made out of gopher wood? Where in the world do we find gopher wood? The answer is: nowhere. There is and was no such thing as gopher wood. What, therefore, was God instructing Noah to build his ark out of? It turns out that gopher in Hebrew sounds an awful lot like the Hebrew word for atonement. It may be that the original writer intended this to be a play on words, indicating that we are to make our arks out of atonements. There is no other known explanation for this. So the story is really telling us that our ark must be made out of atonements, not wood.

I wasn't sure what atonements were exactly and how they would help me see faith. So, I started researching what atoning really was. The bottom line is that atonement means to be at one with or literally to be in tune or in harmony with something. Therefore, atonement not only means to rectify a wrong done to ourselves or others but also to come into harmony with the fact that our wisdom was never meant to make us happy; only faith was. That was when it hit me; my wisdom and I were never in harmony. My wisdom always had a new idea on how to make me happy. My wisdom also tried to make me feel better about my previous attempts to find happiness by reframing, retracting, or rebuking everything in my past that I had done to search for happiness. But as the Bible has told me, my wisdom would never produce happiness, only thorns and thistles that would lead to feelings of shame, fear, worry, sorrow, and desire. My wisdom and I were caught in a vicious cycle. The more my wisdom tried to make me happy, the worse things became. It was no wonder that I came to the point of suicide; I had a tendency to take everything to the extreme and make everything a vicious cycle. The Bible had already given me an example of this predicament in the story of Cain.

Cain and his descendant Lamech were caught in this downward spiral too. I came to the point of suicide, as Lamech had to murder. It was the same vicious cycle with different outcomes but the same result: we were both terminally unhappy. I suppose if we added up all of the mistakes that Cain, Lamech, and I had made searching for peace and rest, we would have enough atonement material to build not one ark but an armada of arks. In the story,

Cain and Lamech never decided to atone for their wisdom's mistakes. They became increasingly defiant, whereas I became increasingly depressed.

I was at a turning point. The Bible and my wisdom were giving me contradictory messages, and I knew that I must choose between them. My suicide attempt was the ultimate event in my life that convinced me that my wisdom would never find me peace and rest. I had hit bottom. The shame I felt after my suicide attempt was my biggest thorn; I erroneously thought suicide would take away my pain, but in reality it only made my suffering worse.[51] I could have carried that shame with me for the rest of my life, but the Noah story told me that there was another way to deal with the shame and find the rest I was so desperately seeking.

At first I didn't have a clue as to how the Noah story was going to help me find faith. I had forgotten everything I had ever known about faith. On the other hand, I was very familiar with my wisdom. After all, I had used my wisdom countless times in the search for happiness. Like Noah's generation, I didn't understand what faith was all about. I wanted to believe the Bible—that faith was the answer to finding rest—but I didn't know it for a fact. I even felt that maybe faith would not be strong enough to take away my shame from the suicide attempt. The thought also came that I was too old to start this undertaking. I should have known better a long time ago and started to build my ark in my twenties, not my forties. Luckily, the Bible had an answer for all my doubts in terms of being too old to recover faith. I don't know why I completely glossed over the fact that Noah was six hundred years old when he started his ark, so compared to Noah, I was in pretty good shape. In due course, I decided that I had nothing more to lose and only happiness to gain, so I kept reading the story of Noah's ark, trying to understand how it related to my life and my faith.

To learn how to get into harmony with our past, we start with Noah's construction of his ark. Noah seemed to have had all his building materials ready at hand. He was a just and perfect man. I don't think the story is telling us that Noah never made a mistake and was perfect in that sense. Rather, I think that when Noah did make a mistake, he atoned for it right away. If he had harmed another person, he made up for it. If he had attempted

51 Depression and suicide are major medical illnesses, and I am not suggesting that they be treated with faith. I am saying that the shame they evoke can only be overcome by atonement.

suicide, I'm sure he would have gone to all his loved ones and asked for their forgiveness.

When I atoned for my suicide with my loved ones, I received a common response of concern for my pain, anger that I had not asked them for help, and guilt that they hadn't known or done something for me themselves. The only other part of atoning for my suicide that I needed to do was to remember what the Bible had told me about my wisdom's mistakes. Atonement isn't about beating ourselves up over our past mistakes; it is about realizing that wisdom can never find peace and rest for us. Only faith can. I was now ready to start construction on my own ark with my first piece of "gopher wood."

Would I have liked an easier way? Sure, but I remember that I had originally determined that I could find my own happiness, peace, and rest in the first place. I had to admit that my wisdom was not capable of making me happy. When I looked around at other people, I asked myself, *Do they know that wisdom won't lead them to peace and rest? Do they care?* Maybe I was the only one in the world who wasn't happy. Would people laugh at my ark even if it was only made out of atonements and not out of visible gopher wood? These were some of the doubts I had, but there was no turning back now.

A funny thing happened when I started to construct my ark. I saw things that had happened to me not as failures but as necessities—as opportunities to build an ark instead of letting my wisdom keep making things worse. I began to feel grateful for all my mistakes. My shame vanished forever, and I knew I was building a place that would lead me to faith. By using my atonement for my suicide attempt as the main keel, and atonements of a lesser degree as the sides and deck of my ark, I became free of the desire to change the things that had happened to me. I even remember joking with a friend that I envisioned my ark as more like a speedboat than an ark and that I would christen it *Suicidal Harmony.*

As we atone for more and more things, our arks become more complete. We remember all the less-than-brilliant things we have tried in our lives in the search for happiness. We no longer need wisdom to solve our past problems because everything we come across in our past fits nicely into our arks. We are even thankful to our past because without our foibles, we could not have built an ark. Of course this is a qualified thankfulness, since if we hadn't foibled with the fruit of the tree of the knowledge of good and evil in the first place, we wouldn't have needed to build arks. But it was not just my mistakes that had gotten in the way of me seeing faith again.

Atoning for my accomplishments was also necessary since they did not bring me happiness, peace, or rest either. For example, my wisdom told me that if I became a doctor, I would be happy and find the fulfillment I was yearning for. Well, that didn't happen. Then my wisdom told me that if I were only a better doctor, I would then be happy—that I needed to study that much harder and then I would be happy. I think we all know where this is leading. So I must atone for becoming a doctor too? Yes, my wisdom had given me many things but not happiness and rest. All my accomplishments would need to become part of my ark, and I could not let my wisdom use them again to make me think that they would lead me to happiness.

Nothing that my wisdom had led me to in my life was wasted; it all went into building a fine ark. Everything I thought was a mistake or an accomplishment turned out to be the perfect ark-building material for *me*. But what exactly does an ark made out of atonements look like, and what does it do? Toward the completion of the ark, I started to understand what I was building. I was building a sanctuary. I visualized a three-dimensional space made out of atonements. I had created a place in my life where my wisdom had no purpose. Once I had atoned for my past, I saw how everything that had happened to me needed to happen for me to build an ark, and my wisdom didn't need to change a thing. I saw my life as unfolding just as it should have, and if I thought that things should have been otherwise, I wouldn't have been able to build my ark. In the end, all my mistakes had created a space in my life where I could stop my wisdom from trying to help me find peace. But what did this space look like?

When we think about Noah's ark, we think of a boat big enough to hold a representative sample of all the animals, but an ark can be any shape. Moses' ark was a basket; the ark of the covenant is usually depicted as a golden box. The Virgin Mary is even called the new ark of the covenant by Catholics. Our ark of atonements is invisible and resides within us. Regardless of their size or shape, arks hold things of great holy value, and what could be more holy than faith?

Remembering from previous chapters that wisdom was the only thing that kept me from faith, it made sense that by building the ark, I had just eliminated the obstacle that had prevented me from experiencing faith.

Once my atonements were in my ark, they could not or need not be changed by wisdom. Now the decision becomes, "Am I brave enough to enter the ark and see what faith is really like?" We have never seen our wisdom at rest; it is always working on something aimed at making us happy. Our wisdom is all we have ever used for our whole lives to try to search for happiness. Abandoning my previous efforts toward the possibility of faith was wonderfully frightening. It was kind of like graduation, knowing that I had outgrown high school but not knowing what the future would bring. These were my first tentative steps back to faith.

At long last, the story of Noah fit with the rest of the primeval history. Adam—man—had decided to grow his own happiness, comfort, and rest, but God knew that man, with only wisdom, not faith, would only produce thorns and thistles, and this failure would lead to feelings of shame, fear, worry, sorrow, and desire. Furthermore, man could not use his wisdom to think his way back to faith. In fact, the more he used his wisdom, the more thorns and thistles and feelings of despair he would produce. It was a vicious cycle that could only be stopped by one thing: building an ark. Although wisdom was good for many things, it was not good for giving us happiness. Wisdom itself could not figure out that it was the only obstacle to faith and the possibility of happiness. We needed to build an ark, an ark out of atonements, to create a sanctuary where we could disarm our wisdom and see what faith was like again.

The Bible does not want us to stop after we have built our ark. It doesn't want us to keep building our ark for the rest of our lives. No, the ark was meant to be used. Once we have built our ark, we can use it to experience faith once again. Genesis 7 shows us how to use the ark to see faith again. But would we recognize faith when we saw it? Once we experienced faith firsthand, would we value faith more than Adam had seemed to in Genesis 3? Adam seemed to have abandoned faith without a second thought.

> It wasn't raining when Noah built the ark.
>
> —Howard Ruff (1931–)[52]

52 ThinkExist.com Quotations. "Howard Ruff quotes". ThinkExist.com Quotations Online 1 Oct. 2012. 20 Nov. 2012 <http://en.thinkexist.com/quotes/howard_ruff/>

Faith is not simply a patience that passively suffers until the storm is past. Rather, it is a spirit that bears things - with resignations, yes, but above all, with blazing, serene hope.
—Corazon Aquino (1933–2009)[53]

Genesis 7

1 And the LORD said unto Noah, Come thou and all thy house into the ark; for thee have I seen righteous before me in this generation.

2 Of every clean beast thou shalt take to thee by sevens, the male and his female: and of beasts that are not clean by two, the male and his female.

3 Of fowls also of the air by sevens, the male and the female; to keep seed alive upon the face of all the earth.

4 For yet seven days, and I will cause it to rain upon the earth forty days and forty nights; and every living substance that I have made will I destroy from off the face of the earth.

5 And Noah did according unto all that the LORD commanded him.

6 And Noah was six hundred years old when the flood of waters was upon the earth.

7 And Noah went in, and his sons, and his wife, and his sons' wives with him, into the ark, because of the waters of the flood.

8 Of clean beasts, and of beasts that are not clean, and of fowls, and of every thing that creepeth upon the earth,

53 Corazon Aquino. BrainyQuote.com, Xplore Inc, 2012. http://www.brainyquote.com/quotes/quotes/c/corazonaqu201108.html, accessed November 21, 2012.

9 There went in two and two unto Noah into the ark, the male and the female, as God had commanded Noah.

10 And it came to pass after seven days, that the waters of the flood were upon the earth.

11 In the six hundredth year of Noah's life, in the second month, the seventeenth day of the month, the same day were all the fountains of the great deep broken up, and the windows of heaven were opened.

12 And the rain was upon the earth forty days and forty nights.

13 In the selfsame day entered Noah, and Shem, and Ham, and Japheth, the sons of Noah, and Noah's wife, and the three wives of his sons with them, into the ark;

14 They, and every beast after his kind, and all the cattle after their kind, and every creeping thing that creepeth upon the earth after his kind, and every fowl after his kind, every bird of every sort.

15 And they went in unto Noah into the ark, two and two of all flesh, wherein is the breath of life.

16 And they that went in, went in male and female of all flesh, as God had commanded him: and the LORD shut him in

17 And the flood was forty days upon the earth; and the waters increased, and bare up the ark, and it was lift up above the earth.

18 And the waters prevailed, and were increased greatly upon the earth; and the ark went upon the face of the waters.

19 And the waters prevailed exceedingly upon the earth; and all the high hills, that were under the whole heaven, were covered.

20 Fifteen cubits upward did the waters prevail; and the mountains were covered.

21 And all flesh died that moved upon the earth, both of fowl, and of cattle, and of beast, and of every creeping thing that creepeth upon the earth, and every man:

22 All in whose nostrils was the breath of life, of all that was in the dry land, died.

23 And every living substance was destroyed which was upon the face of the ground, both man, and cattle, and the creeping things, and the fowl of the heaven; and they were destroyed from the earth: and Noah only remained alive, and they that were with him in the ark.

24 And the waters prevailed upon the earth an hundred and fifty days.

Ultimately, blind faith is the only kind.
—Mason Cooley (1927–2002)[54]

Experiencing Faith Again in the Present

By building an ark, we have learned to see our past in a whole new light and discovered we could not count on our wisdom to bring us happiness. In fact, we knew wisdom would lead us away from peace and rest. Once we have each built our arks, we must know how to best use them. Our next assignment, as it is presented in chapter 7, is even more difficult than building an ark. We must now be willing to board the ark, knowing that we will be leaving behind our past life as we knew it. The flood will destroy everything our wisdom has ever done in the search for happiness. But leaving our past is a frightening decision, even though our wisdom has never found us peace and happiness. It is, after all, the only means we have used to deal with life. We have lived in this world using only our wisdom. We have declared things to be good and things to be evil; we have even used our wisdom to determine our view of what God must be like.

This life based on wisdom was not a terrible life. Look at Cain's family; they had music and tools, they had cities and farms. Wisdom has not made us suffer all the time. We might even have been reasonably happy with the life we had created. The question arises: Do we have to give up all of this just to have faith? What if we give up our old life and don't wind up getting faith? Then we have nothing. That is the risk we must take. We must be totally willing to give up all of our own ideas to see faith again. If any of our old life is left, it will be a gift from God, but we must be ready to have everything taken from us. Entering our ark takes a great deal of courage. This is the topic of chapter 7.

Even though chapter 7 is short and seemingly uncomplicated compared to the other chapters in Genesis, it is the chapter that puts it all together. At first I didn't understand the significance of this chapter; it didn't seem so pivotal. The whole chapter can be stated simply as: Noah got into the ark, and the flood destroyed the world that Noah used to know. Why didn't the

54 Mason Cooley. BrainyQuote.com, Xplore Inc, 2012. http://www.brainyquote.com/quotes/quotes/m/masoncoole394902.html, accessed November 21, 2012.

Bible just add chapter 7 to the end of chapter 6, or an even better idea, to the beginning of chapter 8? Why did the Bible devote a whole chapter to floating in the ark for forty-plus days with nothing happening except for Noah spending a lot of time caring for the animals?

The reason chapter 7 is so important is because it completes the story that tells us how to get faith back in our lives. Chapters 1 through 6 have prepared us to understand chapter 7, just like the six days of creation in Genesis 1 prepared us for the ultimate experience of faith described on the seventh day.

Understanding chapter 7 is not difficult if we know what to look for. The key to understanding this part of the story comes from the very fact that the Bible waited until chapter 7 to give us the answer to getting faith back in our lives. In fact, the number seven is mentioned four times in the first four verses: seventh chapter, seven pairs of clean beasts, seven pairs of clean fowl, and seven days until the flood. Think about hearing a storyteller reciting this opening to an attentive audience; the number seven would certainly stand out. I think the Bible is using the number seven as a clue or an internal link to help us understand the Noah story. It is the ancient Hebrew text's equivalent of the hypertext. If the text were written today on a computer, the number seven would keep popping up in a blue font, beseeching us to click on it. It would be leading us to a common hyperlink. But what does the number seven mean, and to where does it link us?

Seven is the symbol of completion or perfection and also the symbol of rest. Once I recognized that the number seven meant this, I went straight back to the seventh day of creation in the beginning of Genesis 2. Besides the seven pair of clean animals, the seventh day of creation was the only other seven mentioned so far in the primeval history, and I thought there must be a connection. The seventh day of creation certainly represents completion, perfection, and rest. Was the Bible telling me that I should start with day seven of creation and re-read Genesis 2 to understand what was going to happen to Noah in the ark? I think it was; I think that it was another reason why day seven of creation was placed at the beginning of chapter 2 and not found in chapter 1 with the rest of the days of creation. Day seven of creation was cleverly placed at the beginning of chapter 2 to tell us it was the key to understanding chapter 7, urging us to reread and compare Genesis 2 with Genesis 7. We needed to compare the Adam of Genesis 2 with the Noah of

Genesis 7. Once I started rereading Genesis 2, I saw the similarities between the stories of Adam and of Noah. So let's see how the Noah story parallels the creation story in Genesis 2 and what they tell us about faith.

As a review, in the part of Genesis 2 after the seventh day of creation, we saw the Lord God creating the world, man, and the garden of Eden. Man's job was to be the keeper of the garden with its two trees and therefore, by metaphor, a place where faith and wisdom could grow side by side. Once everything was created, a problem soon arose, namely that it was not good that Adam, man, was alone. As Adam and the Lord God set out to fix the problem, the Lord God turned to Adam and told him to name the animals that were being created in the garden. Adam was not to help the Lord God solve the problem of not having a mate; he should first take care of the garden. He should first make sure that his faith was cared for before he thought about solving problems. As Adam named the animals, he was demonstrating to the Lord God that he was being a good keeper of his garden and a good keeper of his faith and that he trusted that a mate would be found. So how does this help us understand the Noah story?

Noah also had a problem that needed to be solved; he had to comfort everyone regarding the curse that the Lord God had placed on the ground for man's sake. He also had a whole slew of animals that needed to be cared for. Noah did exactly as Adam did in concentrating on caring for the animals and showing God that he was the keeper of his faith before anything else. Noah would care for the animals and let God solve the problem of the cursed ground that would only produce thorns and thistles for man.

After God told Noah that a great flood was coming and that he should get into the ark, not another word was spoken between them. There was no explanation as to how rough the flood was going to be or how long it would last. God was not interested in informing Noah as to what to expect. Would the curse be lifted, and what would it be like without a curse? Noah needed only to do his part to take care of the animals, just as Adam did. Remember, Adam had no idea what kind of mate the Lord God had in mind for him. That is where courage comes in; we must be willing to give up control of our lives and humble ourselves and just take care of the animals to show God that we can be the keepers of faith too.

God's solution to the curse of the ground for man's sake came in the form of a flood, and as floods do, it rejuvenated the ground and acted as a symbol of reversing the curse on the ground. We all know that after a flood, the ground is more fertile, but the flood also washes away all of man's achievements. The rushing floodwaters easily erase all human topography and replace it with a thick layer of rich, featureless silt. Since this was a worldwide flood, everything that man had made was washed away. God both solved the problem that Noah's father had foretold and gave Noah a new, clean world in which to live. This is exactly what happened back in Genesis 2; the Lord God solved the problem while Adam took care of the animals. By caring for his faith, Adam simply woke up from surgery and found that everything had been taken care of; he had a perfect mate. Instead of using surgery as He did to solve Adam's problem, God chose to give Noah and his world a gigantic bath. By simply doing what he was told to do—caring for the animals—Noah had a chance for a clean start. Not only was his faith restored, but all the shame, fear, worry, sorrow, and desire from his past life seemed to be washed away too. Noah would not have to use his wisdom to find peace and rest anymore.

What a brilliant metaphor for God solving the problem of the cursed ground and giving Noah a chance to be the keeper of faith at the same time. I had come up with a few alternative metaphors for reversing the curse and helping Noah simultaneously, but I'm not sure they will stand the test of time. In thinking about how to undo the curse of the ground and still save Noah, I first thought of God dropping manure about fifty feet deep over the entire world; that would have rejuvenated the ground and killed most creatures with the breath of life in them except maybe the worms and dung beetles. But there would be no way for even God to allow Noah to come out of that situation smelling like a rose. This might have helped Noah experience faith more fully, but no one would have been able get close enough to him to tell.

The only other idea I had was even worse; I envisioned spraying chemical fertilizers and pesticides over the earth. That would certainly have refortified the ground and would have killed almost everybody, just as God's flood had done, but with chemical burns. Unfortunately, it would also have choked all the waters with a proliferation of algae, and who knows what mutant genes it would have produced? Noah's descendants may have started looking a lot more like *Star Wars* characters than Shem, Ham, and Japheth. All things being considered, I think we should stick to the flood metaphor.

The flood story combines the rejuvenation of the ground with Noah's transformation to experiencing faith again, thus undoing the curse on the ground and washing Noah of the habit of trusting his wisdom to make him happy. Noah could now let faith give him the peace, comfort, and rest for which he had been searching. The flood is not the only metaphor of this type in the Bible. When we think about this kind of transformation to faith, the cleansing metaphor comes up in a variety of forms. Take, for example, Jesus. He went into the desert for a long period of time to cleanse himself of the world and find faith. Jonah had to be swallowed by a whale to understand that he was not in charge of his own fulfillment. We might say that Jesus underwent a dry cleaning process and Jonah endured the spit-and-polish technique. In Noah's case, he was assigned to the rinse-and-hold cycle. They all went through their individual forms of cleansing and in the end were shining examples to us of the keepers of faith.

Using any of these biblical figures, especially Noah and the flood, we can see how to rediscover faith in our lives. We have already learned how to deal with our past with the help of Genesis 6. In this chapter, we have been led to experience faith firsthand in our present life and have been cleansed of our habit of using our wisdom to try to bring us happiness. We had the courage to risk losing everything we thought was true for the opportunity to get faith back in our lives. We risked losing everything we had built in our lives just to glimpse faith again. In the end we realized that the only thing we had lost was our dependence on our wisdom. We had been cleansed of this dependence.

My particular cleansing experience came with the writing of this book. First of all, I'll have to admit that I'm not a writer; I got no better than Bs in high school English, and it probably shows in my colloquial speech and less-than-professional writing style presented in this book. In high school I had no interest in the assignments that I was forced to read, and writing was a chore. I hated doing papers—first, because I could never get down on paper what was in my head. Second, I was lousy at spelling, handwriting, and punctuation. In those days papers had to be hand written, and my mother was the only spelling and grammar checker available. I was much more into math and science, and that's why I became a doctor. Being a doctor, I didn't have to write much, and when I did, I could scribble.

To me thinking about writing a book and getting all my thoughts collected, organized, and written was completely inconceivable, especially if I had to write a book on a topic that was deeply concerning to me—a topic that, in writing, must convey every thought in a way that was clearly understandable. This hurdle in writing was the thing that kept me searching for an answer to faith for so many years; I wanted to find my thoughts in someone else's writings. I did find a lot of writings that started to appeal to me, but in the end, they didn't go far enough, and they left me disappointed. Writing my own book on my own experiences was the only alternative.

As I have said before, once I started writing, I couldn't stop; an hour would go by in a flash. The ideas would easily rush out of my head, but each sentence, each word, and each punctuation mark would get onto paper in a painfully slow process. I would have to jot notes on the side of the paper just so I wouldn't forget the ideas that were coming faster than I could write. The notes became so numerous that they encroached into the space on which I had planned to write the main body of the text. It didn't matter anyway because by the time I needed that space to write, I had invariably lost my original train of thought. Needless to say, my attempt at writing took many writes and rewrites, most of which were handwritten in the bathtub. Later I would type them up and finally go over every word and punctuation mark with a very dear friend and junior high school teacher who was also interested in spiritual matters. She kept me grounded and at least somewhat understandable. I knew if she didn't have a clue as to what I had written, nobody else would either.

If my writings were seen as a cleansing metaphor, as with Noah and the others we have talked about in the Bible, then mine would certainly be viewed as rubbing clean by an eraser. After writing a paragraph, I would erase half of it and start from there. As I incorporated the ideas I had jotted on the sides of my paper, I'd have to erase them too, making more room for new notes. Progress was measured in the number of erasers I went through. When it came right down to it, I believe that this cleansing work of writing a book was the only way that I could have truly experienced faith.

At first it doesn't sound like writing a book is similar to caring for the animals on an ark, but let me try to explain. Instead of caring for the animals, I had to care for my manuscript. Everything I ever thought was true about faith, I wrote down on paper. I subsequently erased all the ideas that turned out to be my misunderstanding of faith. For example, in the beginning, when I first started to read the Bible that my mother had given me, I thought that wisdom was the only thing that could lead me to faith. Figuring out how my wisdom could open a world of faith was all it would take. That is why I tried to understand the different religions of the world. If I could understand the logic of those religions, I was sure that I would be closer to faith.

This paradigm changed when I read about the cherub in Genesis 3. Since I began to see the cherub as representing my own wisdom, I saw that my wisdom was the only thing keeping me from faith; it was certainly not going to help me. I saw myself as Adam standing at the entrance of the garden of Eden. Adam could see the tree of life—the tree of faith—but couldn't get to it. My feelings were exactly the same. I knew my faith was somewhere in my awareness, but I couldn't get closer to it. It felt like an invisible force was holding me back. But come to find out, my wisdom was the very thing that was preventing me from finding faith.

Once I realized the invisible force was my very own wisdom, it loosened its grip on me just a little bit. To relate the feeling I had to Adam's story, it was as if the cherub lost his sword. By stopping my wisdom, I got closer to faith. Noah and Adam stopped their wisdom. They focused on the task at hand and did not try to use their wisdom to directly solve the problem with which each of them were faced. They had faith that God would solve the problem if they did what they were instructed to do—no more, no less. Adam named all the animals, and Noah fed and cleaned up after them.

I did it by cleaning up after my manuscript. The more I erased my old ideas of faith, the more I trusted that the Bible would eventually reveal to me the answers I was looking for, the closer I got to the true faith. I literally had to forget about my quest for faith to let the Bible get me closer to faith. Each time I erased something, I had to let the primeval history fill in the void on the paper. Sometimes I was ready to hear the answer, and sometimes I wasn't. I had to be willing to erase my understanding of the Bible and wait days, weeks, and sometimes years for faith to fill in what I had erased. There was many a time when I wished I had some animals to take care of while I waited for the process to happen, but because I am allergic to cats, dogs, and molds, caring for animals in a stuffy ark was not an option for me.

Everything I needed to know about faith was in the first seven pages of the Bible. I only had to start reading the Bible the way my heart told me to, not the way I thought I should or the way I was told to by people who were using their wisdom to understand the Bible. Just like Noah, I had to be willing to give up all my old ways of doing things to see faith. I had to trust that my heart, not my head or my wisdom, could write this book.

When I wrote with my heart, I had a sense that I was not directing the writing. Rather, once I started writing, the book itself would be in charge of what I paid attention to. I would jump all over the place. Something in chapter 6 would remind me of a better way to word something in chapter 3, and then that would take me to the introduction. This jumping around the chapters of my book made me think of what Noah must have felt like caring for all those animals. I envisioned Noah starting his day by hearing the doves cooing to tell him to feed them, and at the other end of the ark the rattlesnakes would begin rattling, reminding Noah not to forget them, and maybe at the same time Noah would be nudged from the back by an impatient seal. That is what writing this book felt like to me.

As I wrote this book, my experience paralleled Noah's journey in his ark. We both went through a cleansing experience, and we both worked very hard at taking care of the task at hand. In writing this book, I got rid of a lot of ideas I erroneously had about faith. Most of what my wisdom had led me to believe about faith was not true. By writing and following the metaphors in the primeval history, I found that faith was simply meant to give me the peace, comfort, and rest I had been searching for all along.

Taking care of the animals is what the Bible used to symbolize taking care of our garden of Eden, our faith. It had to be a priority over everything else. Adam did it, and so did Noah. To me, writing this book certainly became my number-one priority in life. Writing and erasing became my way of caring for my garden of faith. Erasing my misconceptions on the pages was like pulling the weeds my wisdom had let grow in my garden, all the thorns and thistles. I was not only cleansed, but my garden of faith was also purged of all of the misinformation I had accumulated. Once my garden was cleared, I could really see faith again in my life. It took a lot of time in the bathtub and a lot of erasers for me to see faith. It took me years rather than the days that Noah spent in his ark. With the image of me sitting in a bathtub surrounded by eraser shavings floating on the water, I think we should move quickly to the next chapters, Genesis 8–11.

It takes courage and a lot of hard work to exist in our arks. We risk losing our old ways and work at something that is never easy, just for the chance to re-experience faith. Now there remains but one assignment. We must commit the rest of our lives to faith. Just how Noah committed to this new life and how God's response to it is presented in Genesis 8 through 9:17.

> Our faith comes in moments; our vice is habitual.
>
> —Ralph Waldo Emerson (1803–1882)[55]

55 Ralph Waldo Emerson. BrainyQuote.com, Xplore Inc, 2012. http://www.brainyquote.com/quotes/quotes/r/ralphwaldo397412.html, accessed November 21, 2012.

Faith is the bird that feels the light when the dawn is still dark.
—Rabindranath Tagore (1861–1941)[56]

Genesis 8

1 And God remembered Noah, and every living thing, and all the cattle that was with him in the ark: and God made a wind to pass over the earth, and the waters asswaged;

2 The fountains also of the deep and the windows of heaven
were stopped, and the rain from heaven was restrained;3
And the waters returned from off the earth continually:
and after the end of the hundred and fifty days the waters
were abated.

4 And the ark rested in the seventh month, on the seventeenth day of the month, upon the mountains of Ararat.

5 And the waters decreased continually until the tenth month: in the tenth month, on the first day of the month, were the tops of the mountains seen.

6 And it came to pass at the end of forty days, that Noah opened the window of the ark which he had made:

7 And he sent forth a raven, which went forth to and fro, until the waters were dried up from off the earth.

8 Also he sent forth a dove from him, to see if the waters were abated from off the face of the ground;

9 But the dove found no rest for the sole of her foot, and she returned unto him into the ark, for the waters were on the face of the whole earth: then he put forth his hand, and took her, and pulled her in unto him into the ark.

56 ThinkExist.com Quotations. "Rabindranath Tagore quotes". ThinkExist.com Quotations Online 1 Oct. 2012. 21 Nov. 2012 <http://en.thinkexist.com/quotes/rabindranath_tagore/2.html>

10 And he stayed yet other seven days; and again he sent forth the dove out of the ark;

11 And the dove came in to him in the evening; and, lo, in her mouth was an olive leaf pluckt off: so Noah knew that the waters were abated from off the earth.

12 And he stayed yet other seven days; and sent forth the dove; which returned not again unto him any more.

13 And it came to pass in the six hundredth and first year, in the first month, the first day of the month, the waters were dried up from off the earth: and Noah removed the covering of the ark, and looked, and, behold, the face of the ground was dry.

14 And in the second month, on the seven and twentieth day of the month, was the earth dried.

15 And God spake unto Noah, saying,

16 Go forth of the ark, thou, and thy wife, and thy sons, and thy sons' wives with thee.

17 Bring forth with thee every living thing that is with thee, of all flesh, both of fowl, and of cattle, and of every creeping thing that creepeth upon the earth; that they may breed abundantly in the earth, and be fruitful, and multiply upon the earth.

18 And Noah went forth, and his sons, and his wife, and his sons' wives with him:

19 Every beast, every creeping thing, and every fowl, and whatsoever creepeth upon the earth, after their kinds, went forth out of the ark.

20 And Noah builded an altar unto the LORD; and took of every clean beast, and of every clean fowl, and offered burnt offerings on the altar.

21 And the LORD smelled a sweet savour; and the LORD said in his heart, I will not again curse the ground any more for man's sake; for the imagination of man's heart is evil from his youth; neither will I again smite any more every thing living, as I have done.

22 While the earth remaineth, seedtime and harvest, and cold and heat, and summer and winter, and day and night shall not cease.

Genesis 9:1–17

1 And God blessed Noah and his sons, and said unto them,
Be fruitful, and multiply, and replenish the earth.2 And the
fear of you and the dread of you shall be upon every beast
of the earth, and upon every fowl of the air, upon all that
moveth upon the earth, and upon all the fishes of the sea;
into your hand are they delivered.

3 Every moving thing that liveth shall be meat for you; even as the green herb have I given you all things.

4 But flesh with the life thereof, which is the blood thereof, shall ye not eat.

5 And surely your blood of your lives will I require; at the hand of every beast will I require it, and at the hand of man; at the hand of every man's brother will I require the life of man.

6 Whoso sheddeth man's blood, by man shall his blood be shed: for in the image of God made he man.

7 And you, be ye fruitful, and multiply; bring forth abundantly in the earth, and multiply therein.

8 And God spake unto Noah, and to his sons with him, saying,

9 And I, behold, I establish my covenant with you, and with your seed after you;

10 And with every living creature that is with you, of the fowl, of the cattle, and of every beast of the earth with you; from all that go out of the ark, to every beast of the earth.

11 And I will establish my covenant with you; neither shall all flesh be cut off any more by the waters of a flood; neither shall there any more be a flood to destroy the earth.

12 And God said, This is the token of the covenant which I make between me and you and every living creature that is with you, for perpetual generations:

13 I do set my bow in the cloud, and it shall be for a token of a covenant between me and the earth.

14 And it shall come to pass, when I bring a cloud over the earth, that the bow shall be seen in the cloud:

15 And I will remember my covenant, which is between me and you and every living creature of all flesh; and the waters shall no more become a flood to destroy all flesh.

16 And the bow shall be in the cloud; and I will look upon it, that I may remember the everlasting covenant between God and every living creature of all flesh that is upon the earth.

17 And God said unto Noah, This is the token of the covenant, which I have established between me and all flesh that is upon the earth.

Yea, foolish mortals, Noah's flood is not yet subsided;
two thirds of the fair world it yet covers.
—Herman Melville (1819–1891)[57]

Keeping Faith in Our Future

"And God remembered Noah." When we start reading Genesis 8, we get the idea that God had left Noah in the throes of the flood to fend for himself, and almost as an afterthought, remembered what he had asked Noah to do. But I don't think we should read too much into this opening. I think it merely implies that Noah demonstrated true faith, even when God was not readily at hand. It tells us that Noah did not need God watching his every movement anymore. God did not need to direct Noah as He had done with Adam. Noah had completed his faith journey and was ready to apply faith to every aspect of his life, not just to his life in the ark.

Genesis 8–9:17 finishes Noah's flood story by telling us what we need to do to seal the deal and keep faith going forward. The chapter tells us that there were two aspects to keeping faith in our future. The first was demonstrated when Noah signaled to God that he was ready to leave the ark, and the second was when God gave Noah a new blessing of prosperity and a new covenant of faith. Let's begin with how Noah signaled to God that he was ready to live a life outside his ark with faith giving him the comfort, peace, and rest he needed.

> And it came to pass at the end of forty days, that Noah opened the window of the ark which he had made: And he sent forth a raven, which went forth to and fro, until the waters were dried up from off the earth. Also he sent forth a dove from him, to see if the waters were abated from off the face of the ground; But the dove found no rest for the sole of her foot, and she returned unto him into the ark, for the waters were on the face of the whole earth: then he put forth his hand, and took her, and pulled her in unto him

57 ThinkExist.com Quotations. "Herman Melville quotes". ThinkExist.com Quotations Online 1 Oct. 2012. 20 Nov. 2012 <http://en.thinkexist.com/quotes/herman_melville/6.html>

> into the ark. And he stayed yet other seven days; and again he sent forth the dove out of the ark; And the dove came in to him in the evening; and, lo, in her mouth was an olive leaf pluckt off: so Noah knew that the waters were abated from off the earth. And he stayed yet other seven days; and sent forth the dove; which returned not again unto him any more. (Gen. 8:6–12)

By verse 8, Noah had been in the ark for a considerable length of time. He had proven that he could care for the animals, and by analogy, he had proven that he could care for his faith. What better way to tell God that he was ready to live a life filled with faith than to send animal messengers? Noah logically chose birds because they could fly above the earth in the open firmament of heaven. So Noah sent forth a raven and a dove. Why did Noah release two different birds, and why did they behave differently?

Before we talk about the birds, let's reexamine how the knowledge of good and evil had gotten us into the mess that we were in. In Genesis 2 and 3, we were given two gifts: faith and the knowledge of good and evil. In this book, we have used the term *wisdom* to stand in for the knowledge of good and evil. Other metaphors in the story have told us that we need to tend our garden and the animals, using our knowledge of good and evil, our wisdom. If we tended our garden well, then both trees would grow and prosper. Our wisdom was not just meant for taking care of our faith. No, it was also intended for us to use to see all the complexities of the world, all the good and all the evil. But seeing all of this good and evil would overwhelm us if we could not rest from it too. That is why we were given faith, to rest from all that our wisdom can experience in the world.

The Bible had already told us that this world wasn't perfect; it was better than perfect. Humans could see all the complexities the imperfect world had to offer, and they also had a resting place away from these complexities. The story continued by telling us not to abandon faith. If we abandon faith, then we would have to live a life of constant turmoil and be in a perpetual search for a resting place that we would never find outside of faith. We would be bound to seeing all the good and evil without a resting place. The Bible told us that this is what happened when Adam and Eve ate from the tree of the knowledge of good and evil. This act represents not only abandoning faith to give us rest, but it also makes the point that we ask our wisdom to find us our own peace and rest, something that wisdom was never meant to do. In a very real sense, we bound our wisdom to the task of finding us happiness. We too were bound because we had abandoned faith and relied too heavily on our knowledge of good and evil to try to find us the comfort we had lost. Time after time we found ourselves following our wisdom to what we thought might be happiness; but in the end there was only disappointment, thorns, and thistles, as the Bible tells us. So now let's see what the releasing of the birds symbolizes.

To me, the black and the white birds taken together represent the knowledge of good and evil or wisdom. The birds represent wisdom, with one added characteristic—wisdom that is still bound to Noah. The birds are still in the ark, dependent on Noah for sustenance, and do not fly freely. Noah has found faith, and that will bring him peace, but he still hasn't set his wisdom free from the task of giving him happiness too. Noah could have been thinking, *Why not try to keep control of both faith and wisdom?* It was not that Noah was using his birds, his wisdom, to bring him happiness anymore, but why not keep them in his back pocket, so to speak, just in case he needed to use them again? But of course, we know this will not work, and Noah knew this too. By releasing the birds, Noah was symbolically setting his wisdom free from the task of trying to make him happy permanently. Noah would find peace, comfort, and rest in faith and faith alone.

Now I'll admit that this appears like Noah was giving up his knowledge of good and evil totally, but he was not. We cannot give up our ability to think any more than we can choose not to breathe; but we can free our thinking of trying to find us happiness, peace, and rest. Once free of this burden, we can use our wisdom to follow the instruction that we were initially given to have this peace, comfort, and rest. By releasing the birds, Noah gave a symbol that he would not control his wisdom as he saw fit; he would simply use it to follow God's instructions. Noah would use his wisdom to tend his garden of Eden, and if he had any time left over, he would marvel at all the complexities of the world. That would have been all there was to the story if it weren't for the dove.

Noah set both the raven and the dove free, but the dove came back to Noah twice. Was that implying that it was harder to give up the knowledge of good than it was to give up the knowledge of evil, assuming that the black raven represented the knowledge of evil and the white dove represented the knowledge of good? I think there is something to this. I used to think that if I did good works, it would not only give me happiness but also would get me in good graces with God. I found that what I deemed as good and what I did as good still never brought me the happiness for which I was searching.

I remember when I decided to become a doctor and devote my life to helping people with asthma. That was a very good decision, and I hope that I have helped many people, but it has never given me the peace, comfort, and rest for which I was searching. I imagine that is what Noah was asking himself too, when the dove came back to him the first time. Noah thought about it for seven days and decided that even the knowledge of good and doing good works would not give him the peace that faith would, and he sent forth the dove again.

The second time the dove came back, it had an olive leaf in its beak. Supposedly the leaf showed Noah that the ground was drying up, but was the olive leaf really a sign from God that He had finally accepted that Noah was ready to free both the knowledge of evil and the knowledge of good from the burden of finding him happiness? I think this was the exact message being sent to Noah. Once Noah knew the knowledge of good would not bring him happiness, he released the dove one last time, and the dove *returned not again unto him anymore.*

Throughout the ages, the olive branch has symbolized peace. It should not be overlooked that when Noah did give up control of the knowledge of both good and evil, it was then that God sent him a symbol of peace in the form of an olive leaf. What better peace is there than the peace we get from faith? If we insist on taking the story only literally, the olive branch would have become just the symbol of things that were dried, like the land after the flood, and then we would find olive branches on the logos of hair dryers, towels, and food dehydrators, not to mention antidiarrheal remedies.

Now let's move back to the storyline. Once Noah had confirmed dry land and left the ark, he built an altar and sacrificed one of every clean animal. What is this sacrifice in Genesis 8 trying to tell us? Noah already told the Lord that he was ready to start a new life with the releasing of the birds. At first I was confused as to why the altar and offerings were included in the story. Why did Noah have to build an altar, having just released the birds to show God that he was ready to have faith back in his life? I think the answer is that the sacrifice is another hyperlink to tell us how to interpret the next part of the story. Now, if chapter 7 is a hyperlink to day seven of creation, Noah's offering must link us back to Genesis 4, where Cain and Abel made the first offering to God. But before we reread Genesis 4, let's finish off the last few verses of Genesis 8.

In these verses we are given a glimpse of what God was thinking to Himself in His heart.

> And the LORD smelled a sweet savour; and the LORD said in his heart, I will not again curse the ground any more for man's sake; for the imagination of man's heart is evil from his youth; neither will I again smite any more every thing living, as I have done. (Gen. 8:21)

Here God is telling us not that humans were evil from the get-go but rather that our imaginations would constantly try to convince us that we could deal with good and evil ourselves; we did not need faith. From our youth, we will try to use our wisdom to bring us true peace and happiness. In these verses, God is warning Noah not to listen to his wisdom again if it is trying to bring peace, happiness and rest. Even going through a flood won't permanently prevent our wisdom from seeking to try to bring us happiness again and again.

In His thoughts, God had decided that He could not keep convincing man to see the value of faith. Besides, God's batting average was not all that impressive; for the ten generations of humans from Adam to Noah (with the curse on the ground), God had only managed to convert two humans to a life of faith: Enoch and Noah. No, God would not waste His time on this project anymore; if humans really wanted faith, they would have to help each other. God would wait for those individuals that had decided to make the journey back to faith.

The Bible ends chapter 8 with a poem in which God commits to never destroying the earth again and to an enduring cycle of opposites. I believe that this poem is meant as a guide to all of humanity. It tells us that there will be an unending cycle of opposites in store for us. Like the roller coaster I have mentioned in a previous chapter, with its ups and downs, life will consist of this unending cycle until we realize that hidden in the poem, at the very end, is the word *Sabbath* (Sabbath is translated as cease in this case). Of course Sabbath is the seventh day and the day of rest with God. It tells us that this cycle will not stop as long as the earth survives, but whenever we tire of this endless cycle, we can find rest in the end, in Sabbath, in faith.

> While the earth remaineth,
> seedtime and harvest,
> and cold and heat,
> and summer and winter,
> and day and night
> shall not cease.

As we finish Genesis 8 and God's conversation with Himself and move into Genesis 9, we find God blessing Noah. The blessing is so important that it is repeated in the text:

> And God blessed Noah and his sons, and said unto them, Be fruitful, and multiply, and replenish the earth. (Gen. 9:1)

> And you [Noah], be ye fruitful, and multiply; bring forth abundantly in the earth, and multiply therein. (Gen. 9:7)

This was a new blessing that was presented to Noah and all of humanity with some very old ideas. Both versions remind us of God's initial blessing that He gave His newly created humans on day six of creation in Genesis 1.

> And God blessed them, and God said unto them, Be fruitful, and multiply, and replenish the earth, and subdue it: and have dominion over the fish of the sea, and over the fowl of the air, and over every living thing that moveth upon the earth. And God said, Behold, I have given you every herb bearing seed, which is upon the face of all the earth, and every tree, in the which is the fruit of a tree yielding seed; to you it shall be for meat. And to every beast of the earth, and to every fowl of the air, and to every thing that creepeth upon the earth, wherein there is life, I have given every green herb for meat: and it was so. And God saw every thing that he had made, and, behold, it was very good.

> And the evening and the morning were the sixth day. (Gen. 1:28–31)

God also informs Noah that man was in charge of everything worldly; the only thing that they were not in charge of was faith. It is obvious that God did not need the world of good and evil, the world that He had just given to man. He'd seen it all before; He had been there and done that. God seemed to seek only one thing: faith. When we think about it, God could have easily kept all the faith to Himself. He alone could have had a very nice resting place away from all the ups and downs of the universe, but He wanted to share His faith with creatures that could/would cherish it as much as He did. So God gave us control of all things in anticipation that we would share with Him our faith.

God did take away one thing from Noah. Gone was the symbol of caring for the animals; they now live in fear of humans. It seems that Noah must now show his commitment to faith in terms of how he deals with the blood of animals and humans.

> And the fear of you and the dread of you shall be upon every beast of the earth, and upon every fowl of the air, upon all that moveth upon the earth, and upon all the fishes of the sea; into your hand are they delivered. Every moving thing that liveth shall be meat for you; even as the green herb have I given you all things. But flesh with the life thereof, which is the blood thereof, shall ye not eat. And surely your blood of your lives will I require; at the hand of every beast will I require it, and at the hand of man; at the hand of every man's brother will I require the life of man. Whoso sheddeth man's blood, by man shall his blood be shed: for in the image of God made he man. (Gen. 9:2–6)

I can see why these verses have led to dietary customs like draining the blood from animals completely before cooking. It also led to arguments for capital punishment. But I have to believe that the Bible is using blood and the shedding of blood symbolically, just like caring for animals was a symbol for caring for faith. This view becomes clear when we look at 9:4 a little more closely:

> But flesh with the life thereof, which is the blood thereof, shall ye not eat.

Here we find the symbolism. The blood represents life. But the word *life* can mean many different things. If it means the physical body, then I can see the reasoning behind the banning of eating blood and the punishment for murder. But I think that a literal meaning is the wrong take here. The Hebrew word for life in this and subsequent verses means the soul of an animal or human. The soul should be respected. It is not our physical life that blood is a symbol for; it is our spiritual life, our faith.

To understand these verses even more, we can use our hyperlink of Noah's offering to take us back to the only other section of the primeval history where not only were offerings made but blood was mentioned, in Genesis 4. Let's reread the hyperlink.

> And in process of time it came to pass, that Cain brought of the fruit of the ground an offering unto the LORD. And Abel, he also brought of the firstlings of his flock and of the fat thereof. And the LORD had respect unto Abel and to his offering: But unto Cain and to his offering he had not respect. And Cain was very wroth, and his countenance fell. And the LORD said unto Cain, Why art thou wroth? and why is thy countenance fallen? If thou doest well, shalt thou not be accepted? and if thou doest not well, sin lieth at the door. And unto thee shall be his desire, and thou shalt rule over him. And Cain talked with Abel his brother: and it came to pass, when they were in the field, that Cain rose up against Abel his brother, and slew him. And the LORD said unto Cain, Where is Abel thy brother? And he said, I know not: Am I my brother's keeper? And he said, What hast thou done? the voice of thy brother's blood crieth unto me from the ground. And now art thou cursed from the earth, which hath opened her mouth to receive thy brother's blood from thy hand; When thou tillest the ground, it shall not henceforth yield unto thee her strength; a fugitive and a vagabond shalt thou be in the earth. And Cain said unto the LORD, My punishment is greater than I can bear. Behold,

> thou hast driven me out this day from the face of the earth; and from thy face shall I be hid; and I shall be a fugitive and a vagabond in the earth; and it shall come to pass, that every one that findeth me shall slay me. And the LORD said unto him, Therefore whosoever slayeth Cain, vengeance shall be taken on him sevenfold. And the LORD set a mark upon Cain, lest any finding him should kill him. And Cain went out from the presence of the LORD, and dwelt in the land of Nod, on the east of Eden. (Gen. 4:3–16)

I don't think it is a coincidence that there are only two places where an offering to God was made and the topic of blood comes up within a few verses. So what can we gather from the story about Abel's blood and that of the blood in Genesis 9? First of all, Abel's blood had a voice and cried. We also know from our discussion of Genesis 4 that Abel symbolically represents the faith side of us. Abel, faith, soul, and blood are metaphorically one and the same. So the blood is the soul and is the faith of an individual and must be respected and supported. In these verses, we are told never to spill or damage someone else's soul. Even though I'm sure God was concerned with people not killing each other, I'll bet He was more concerned that people not harm other people's souls.

Now when it comes to shedding human blood, we don't have to restrict ourselves to legalities (such as dietary laws and capital punishment). We can read the verses as a warning for us to heed. Do not spill the blood or harm the faith or soul of your brother because in the end your faith will be harmed as much, if not more, than theirs. Once again, think of the Cain and Abel story. Cain's life was devoid of faith after he spilled Abel's blood, his faith. For shedding his brother's blood, Cain must live the rest of his life without faith; he shall be forever hidden from the face of God. All of Cain's faith had been spilled because he had spilled his brother's. In fact, Cain was protected from dying lest his killer suffer sevenfold. Cain was not even allowed to die to end his suffering. This interpretation—that we must equate blood with faith—makes a whole lot more sense than to think that God, in Genesis 9:4, from out of the blue, started to be concerned about spilling the literal blood of animals and man.

We have just discovered that "blood" is the new symbol for our faith, and it seems, on first reading, that God requires this blood. In the KJV, the Hebrew word that was translated into *require* leads us to think in terms of payment rather than being something that would please or satisfy God. In other words, we take these verses to mean that God has given us everything in the world and for that we need to pay God in the currency of faith. I am thinking the word *require* is perhaps too narrow of a translation and has given us the idea that we must pay God in blood for all the other things that He has given us. Personally, I can't imagine that God requires us to pay Him anything. God can't really require animal or human blood, can He? How can God even require our faith? (In this case, faith is not defined as a choice of beliefs but as a deep bonding and resting in and with God.) If faith is "required," then it can't be faith. It can be loyalty, but can it, by any stretch of the imagination, be considered faith?

With these questions in mind, we need to examine the original text a little closer. If we look at the Hebrew word that had been translated as require, it appears that an equally valid translation would be the word *seek*. The word *seek* gives a better feel to the verses. God seeks our faith, He does not require or demand our faith, and faith is the only thing that satisfies Him. To see how this would change the intent of these verses, I have changed the word *blood* into the word *faith* and the word *require* into the word *seek*. Now we can read this temporary alteration of the Bible.

> And surely your *faith* will I *seek*; at the hand of every beast will I *seek* it, and at the hand of man; at the hand of every man's brother will I *seek* the *faith* of man. Whoso sheddeth man's *faith*, by man shall his *faith* be shed: for in the image of God made the man. (Gen. 9:5–6)

With these temporary changes, it almost sounds like God is asking us to share in faith with Him rather than seeing faith as a law or a payment that is required. I can imagine God inviting us to rest with Him on the seventh day of creation, just as He had planned. The following engraved invitation might read:

GOD SEEKS YOUR COMPANY

FOR A PROFOUND EXPERIENCE OF

PEACE, COMFORT AND REST.

LOCATION: SEVENTH DAY OF CREATION

Next we are told that God blessed Noah and again promised not to destroy the world or cause a great flood. This is nice for the world. But wait a minute—the only reason Noah needed to build an ark was because a great flood was coming. By metaphor, this is how Noah found his faith. So if God is no longer going to cause a flood in our lives, then how are we supposed to get faith back for ourselves? Not to worry, we have Noah's story to act as a guide; besides, with our wisdom in full search of happiness, we will cause plenty of storms and floods in our lives by ourselves. We don't need God's help to get into trouble. Just because God doesn't cause a flood in my life doesn't mean I won't have one; it simply means He wasn't behind it.

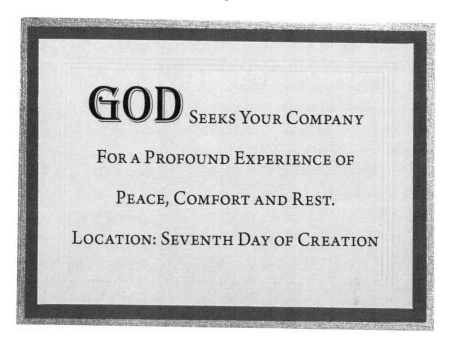

The Bible is telling us not to expect God to be as apparent in our lives as He was in Adam's and Noah's lives, directing them on their every move. We must also remember that we don't have to necessarily see our journey back to faith in terms of surviving a flood; any cleansing metaphor will do. Jesus was dry cleaned, Jonah was polished, and I was erased. We all have to find our own cleansing metaphor, but we can still use the original flood as a prototypical cleansing example. What these verses are telling us is that once we have gone through our flood—that is, dealt with our past and became cleansed of the idea of using our wisdom to find happiness—then we will never have to do that again. We won't have to keep building or repairing our ark before the next flood comes. We won't have to spend any more time in the desert, the whale, or the bathtub again. Well, maybe I should continue to spend some time in the bathtub. What God is telling us is that we have passed the flood stage in our sojourn back to faith, and we will get new instructions.

The next part of the story tells us that God set his bow, a rainbow, in the sky after a storm. This was a symbol of His covenant, but what does it mean? The new covenant will give us new instructions on how to live our lives, but for now let's focus on what the rainbow represented to Noah, having just gone through the flood. To Noah, it meant that he would never have to undergo the extreme cleansing process he underwent in the flood. I believe God set the rainbow in the sky to remind Noah of one very important thing. The rainbow after the storm reminded Noah that even though a flood would not come again, he would still have to face many storms in his life, many challenges of adversity and misery. Noah's imagination will be tempted again to try to find its own peace, comfort, and rest. His wisdom will jump to the ready to try and fix everything to make him feel better. Noah must not let his wisdom do this but must have trust that faith will supply the rainbow. Noah will find peace, comfort, and rest in the rainbow that comes at the end of storms. More about the dark storms and the bright rainbows will be discussed in the next chapter.

The rest of chapter 9 and chapters 10 and 11 show us how to work with our faith in the real world after we leave our ark. The chapters contain two stories separated by family genealogies of the three sons of Noah. The two stories—Noah's curse on his grandson and the Tower of Babel—may at first not seem like powerful stories about how we can put our faith into action, but we will see that they most certainly are.

> By faith Abel offered unto God By faith Enoch was translated that he should not see death; ... By faith Noah ... became heir of the righteousness which is by faith. (Heb. 11:4–5, 7)

Chapter 5

The Practice Maintaining a Healthy Faith through Action

Introduction to Faith in Action

Faith is not belief. Belief is passive. Faith is active.
—Edith Hamilton (1867–1963)[58]

CHAPTERS 9 THROUGH 11 OF Genesis explain the phrase "faith without works is dead." It takes work to keep faith in our lives. If we see the primeval history marking out the stages of the development of faith in our lives, then the final achievement is keeping faith alive in our everyday activities. Let's review the stages and the pitfalls explained so far. We all start out in the garden of Eden, naked and not ashamed. We have both faith and wisdom, like the two trees, and they are vital in our lives. But from our

58 ThinkExist.com Quotations. "Edith Hamilton quotes". ThinkExist.com Quotations Online 1 Oct. 2012. 20 Nov. 2012 <http://en.thinkexist.com/quotes/edith_hamilton/>

youth, we humans have a tendency to abandon faith and use our wisdom to search for our own happiness, peace, and rest. We ask our wisdom to find us peace, comfort, and rest, something that wisdom was never meant to do. Yet we persist in this folly, most of us for our entire lives. Still in our hearts we remember what life with faith and wisdom was meant to be like. It pulls at our being, whether we recognize it or not.

All we must first do is ask the question, "How do I get faith back in my life?" For us in the Western world, the answer has been written down and preserved as the primeval history in the Bible. If we are to get faith back in our lives, we must build an ark out of our atonements for the misadventures we have had on our self-determined search for happiness, peace, and rest. We must be willing to give up everything our wisdom has accomplished in this world. We must be willing to be totally cleansed to see the faith we knew when we were naked and not ashamed. Once we have faith back in our lives, we must use it or we will lose it again. We must trust that the Bible will help us no matter what stage we are at in the quest for faith. Let's see how the next chapters reinforce these ideas.

> He who has faith has ... an inward reservoir of courage, hope, confidence, calmness and assuring trust that all will come out well—even though to the world it may appear to come out most badly.
>
> —B. C. Forbes (1880–1954)[59]

59 ThinkExist.com Quotations. "B. C. Forbes quotes". ThinkExist.com Quotations Online 1 Oct. 2012. 21 Nov. 2012 <http://en.thinkexist.com/quotes/b._c._forbes/>

Faith means living with uncertainty—feeling your way through life, letting your heart guide you like a lantern in the dark.
—Dan Millman (1946–)[60]

Genesis 9

1 And God blessed Noah and his sons, and said unto them, Be fruitful, and multiply, and replenish the earth.2 And the fear of you and the dread of you shall be upon every beast of the earth, and upon every fowl of the air, upon all that moveth upon the earth, and upon all the fishes of the sea; into your hand are they delivered.

3 Every moving thing that liveth shall be meat for you; even as the green herb have I given you all things.

4 But flesh with the life thereof, which is the blood thereof, shall ye not eat.

5 And surely your blood of your lives will I require; at the hand of every beast will I require it, and at the hand of man; at the hand of every man's brother will I require the life of man.

6 Whoso sheddeth man's blood, by man shall his blood be shed: for in the image of God made he man.

7 And you, be ye fruitful, and multiply; bring forth abundantly in the earth, and multiply therein.

8 And God spake unto Noah, and to his sons with him, saying,

9 And I, behold, I establish my covenant with you, and with your seed after you;

60 ThinkExist.com Quotations. "Dan Millman quotes". ThinkExist.com Quotations Online 1 Oct. 2012. 20 Nov. 2012 <http://en.thinkexist.com/quotes/Dan_Millman/>

10 And with every living creature that is with you, of the fowl, of the cattle, and of every beast of the earth with you; from all that go out of the ark, to every beast of the earth.

11 And I will establish my covenant with you; neither shall all flesh be cut off any more by the waters of a flood; neither shall there any more be a flood to destroy the earth.

12 And God said, This is the token of the covenant which I make between me and you and every living creature that is with you, for perpetual generations:

13 I do set my bow in the cloud, and it shall be for a token of a covenant between me and the earth.

14 And it shall come to pass, when I bring a cloud over the earth, that the bow shall be seen in the cloud:

15 And I will remember my covenant, which is between me and you and every living creature of all flesh; and the waters shall no more become a flood to destroy all flesh.

16 And the bow shall be in the cloud; and I will look upon it, that I may remember the everlasting covenant between God and every living creature of all flesh that is upon the earth.

17 And God said unto Noah, This is the token of the covenant, which I have established between me and all flesh that is upon the earth.

18 And the sons of Noah, that went forth of the ark, were Shem, and Ham, and Japheth: and Ham is the father of Canaan.

19 These are the three sons of Noah: and of them was the whole earth overspread.

20 And Noah began to be an husbandman, and he planted a vineyard:

21 And he drank of the wine, and was drunken; and he was uncovered within his tent.

22 And Ham, the father of Canaan, saw the nakedness of his father, and told his two brethren without.

23 And Shem and Japheth took a garment, and laid it upon both their shoulders, and went backward, and covered the nakedness of their father; and their faces were backward, and they saw not their father's nakedness.

24 And Noah awoke from his wine, and knew what his younger son had done unto him.

25 And he said, Cursed be Canaan; a servant of servants shall he be unto his brethren.

26 And he said, Blessed be the LORD God of Shem; and Canaan shall be his servant.

27 God shall enlarge Japheth, and he shall dwell in the tents of Shem; and Canaan shall be his servant.

28 And Noah lived after the flood three hundred and fifty years.

29 And all the days of Noah were nine hundred and fifty years: and he died.

JUST LIKE MANY OTHER SECTIONS of Genesis, the first part of chapter 9 functions in two ways. The first is to finalize the flood story by blessing Noah and giving him a new covenant, which is why I included it with chapter 8. The second function of the first part of Genesis 9 is to introduce us to the works of faith—what we need to do to keep faith in our lives. Genesis 9 couples a blessing and a covenant to get us started in our new lives.

In Genesis 8, we saw that Noah had regained his faith and was ready to start a new life from the beginning, from scratch. Noah was cleansed of the idea that his wisdom could bring him happiness. It seems as though God was ready to start over too. God would not again curse the ground or cause a flood. God would not coax man back to faith anymore. In Genesis 9, God blesses Noah and gives new instructions on how to live a life filled with faith.

These new instructions are not at all like the old instructions we saw in Genesis 2. The old directives informed Adam to be the keeper of the garden of Eden, including tending to the animals and not eating of the fruit of the tree of the knowledge of good and evil. Of course, Noah knew nothing about the old instructions; Noah thought the past was filled with giants and marriages between sons of gods and daughters of men. But Noah had witnessed the un-cursing of the ground and his own cleansing of the idea that wisdom could bring him rest. In Noah's new world, God was not going to curse the ground anymore or cause a flood, but He was also not going to plant a garden with two special trees for Noah to care for. The animals now lived in fear of Noah rather than being in need of his care. Without the garden of Eden, Noah was on his own to preserve the faith in his life. Nevertheless, Noah knew much more than Adam did about faith and what it was like to live without it. Noah also knew what it took to get faith back in his life. So God gave Noah new instructions, a new covenant to live by. Three verses tell Noah all he needs to know to keep faith alive in his life:

> But flesh with the life thereof, which is the blood thereof, shall ye not eat. And surely your blood of your lives will I require; at the hand of every beast will I require it, and at the hand of man; at the hand of every man's brother will I require the life of man. Whoso sheddeth man's blood, by man shall his blood be shed: for in the image of God made he man. (Gen. 9:4–6)

We have already learned that *blood* in these verses is the new symbol of faith and God does not require our faith as we generally interpret the meaning of the word *require*. God seeks our faith rather than demanding it in payment, as we might have thought. The words that are important in understanding what these verses are telling us to do to keep faith in our life are "the hand of man." The hand of man quite simply refers to everything we do. Whether we use our hands to accomplish what we set out to do or "lend a hand" to help others, it must be done remembering that God seeks our faith and our faith alone. When we eat, play, or work, we must remember this. In addition to remembering faith in everything we do, we must also not harm the faith of others, lest our faith be shed.

The Bible is telling us that once we have faith back in our lives, we need to remember it in everything we do. To help us remember, God placed a rainbow in the clouds as a token of this new covenant. The story tells us that when God sees the rainbow in the sky, He will remember this covenant, but is God placing a rainbow in the sky to remind Himself of a new covenant with man? I hardly think so. God wasn't the one who forgot about the first covenant; man was. No, God placed clouds and a rainbow in the sky to give *us* a reminder. The clouds and rainbow tell us exactly what to remember about faith. Since a rainbow is made out of light, I can't help but think that it is another hyperlink to the first part of Genesis 1 that talks about light. Furthermore, clouds and rainbows are signs of nature, and we know that Genesis 1 uses nature to describe the characteristics of faith. So how do clouds and rainbows fit into this scheme? Well, clouds are associated with storms, darkness, and destruction; rainbows, as we have said, are made of light. I think we all know where we are headed—yes, right back to the first day of creation with the darkness separated from the light.

> And God said, Let there be light: and there was light. And God saw the light, that good: and God divided the light from the darkness. And God called the light Day, and the darkness he called Night. And the evening and the morning were the first day. (Gen. 1:3–5)

There was darkness and there was light. The light was separated from the darkness, and the light was good. The storms in Genesis 9, just like the darkness, simply represent the misery and adversity we find in life. The light and the rainbow are symbols of the faith we have in our lives, and they are separate from the darkness. Genesis 9 is using nature to symbolize faith, just as we see in chapter 1. Instead of faith being described by the seven days of creation in chapter 1, we see faith represented as the separate colors of the rainbow. We can use the image of clouds and rainbows as representing what

God wants us to remember about faith. There will be misery and adversity in our lives, but there will also be faith. Faith is separate from the rest of our lives and gives us peace, comfort, and rest from the adversities. When we face trouble, we need to look for the rainbow.

The first part of chapter 9 has told us several things about faith in action. Faith is something that can easily be lost; we cannot take it for granted. We must remember it in all our daily activities. We must not harm the faith of others, and we must also not let our wisdom start its own search for its own peace, comfort, and rest. Noah would also have to use his gift of wisdom and his gift of faith without God's direct involvement; it was up to Noah to decide what he should and shouldn't do.

Genesis 9:18–29 tells a story about Noah and his family after the flood. It is a story where we can either judge Noah in the harshest of terms or see how it fits in with the rest of the primeval history as an example of how Noah put his faith into action. Let's go through the story a few verses at a time, remembering to constantly relate it to ideas we have already discovered in Genesis.

> And the sons of Noah, that went forth of the ark, were Shem, and Ham, and Japheth: and Ham is the father of Canaan. These are the three sons of Noah: and of them was the whole earth overspread. (Gen. 9:18–19)

These verses make sure we know the characters. It introduces one new person, Noah's grandson and Ham's son, Canaan. The fact that Canaan was mentioned at the beginning of the story implies that some time had elapsed since the flood. We will find out in Genesis 10 that Canaan is Ham's fourth son, and unless Ham's wife delivered quadruplets on the ark, several seasons must have passed before Canaan was born. Nothing is said about what kind of a child Canaan was, but I can't help but to think that from the sound of his name, he was at least a little like Adam's son, Cain.

It is also very apparent that God is not physically present as He was in prior chapters. Now that we know the people who are involved in the story, we can start to find out what happened.

> And Noah began to be an husbandman, and he planted a vineyard: And he drank of the wine, and was drunken; and he was uncovered within his tent. (Gen. 9:20–21)

Here we have two short verses that cause us to have more questions than answers. Why did Noah decide to be a farmer at his age, and why weren't his three sons supporting him? Was the vineyard the whole garden or just a small part? When did Noah learn how to make wine? Was this the first time Noah was drunk? If Noah was a drinker, then he probably wasn't all that perfect in his generation. Why does this story mention such an undistinguished event such as Noah getting drunk and being uncovered in his tent? Noah is supposed to be a hero, a person of great faith, so why does the story portray him in such ordinary terms? The list of questions could go on, but I think it is best to see these verses in another light—the light of the rest of the primeval history.

To understand the logic of these verses, let's look at it backward. We'll start at the last few words and work our way to the beginning. We find Noah naked in his tent. To know what this might mean, we need to look for other references to nakedness and what they might imply. In Genesis 3, nakedness was the first thing Adam and Eve noticed after eating of the fruit of the tree of the knowledge of good and evil. The Bible says they were afraid because they were naked. I don't think that in Noah's case he was suffering from any fear. He may have suffered from a little hangover in the morning, but he would not suffer from fear. Therefore, Adam and Eve's nakedness after they ate from the tree of the knowledge of good and evil does not seem to fit Noah's situation.

The only other nakedness that is mentioned is found at the end of Genesis 2, when Adam and Eve were naked and not ashamed. This stands in complete contrast to the nakedness found in Genesis 3. I think we are on to something with the second example. Noah, after he had rediscovered faith, and Adam and Eve, before they ate from the tree of the knowledge of good and evil, were both comfortable in faith and with themselves. They had nothing to hide. In terms of how the author of the stories tells us this, it is easy to see that Adam and Eve could legitimately show their nakedness to each other since they were mates, not to mention the only two humans in existence. Noah, on the other hand, could not just strut around the family camp naked in front of his daughters-in-law. It wouldn't work today, and I'm sure it would have sent the wrong message to the people listening to the recited Bible thousands of years ago too. Noah's wife and sons would have probably thought the flood had pushed Noah mentally over the edge. The author of Genesis had to be very careful as to how to portray Noah not being ashamed of his nakedness. It was a brilliant idea on the author's part to have Noah get drunk and expose himself in his tent. The point to us is made that Noah was naked and not ashamed; it occurred in a socially acceptable way, allowing no one to think he was out of line.

Now let's take another step backward. The story tells us that Noah made some wine from his garden and got drunk. Here we have another hyperlink; Noah was in a garden. The curse of the ground had been lifted, and Noah planted a garden. This verse is telling us that Noah had planted his own garden, just like God had planted the garden of Eden. Now I'm not saying that Noah created the garden of Eden, but the story is telling us that Noah had returned to a state of being that was described in the garden of Eden. It was a state of being where he could enjoy both faith and wisdom, and he knew exactly for what each was meant. What better definition of our own garden of Eden could we ask for?

It is not the difference between Noah's garden and the original garden of Eden that is important here. It is the difference between Noah's garden and the ones Adam and Cain were trying to grow that is crucial. Remember that both Adam and Cain were alienated from the ground and could grow only thorns and thistles that made them feel shame, fear, worry, sorrow, and desire. Noah's garden was not cursed; he grew healthy trees, and he had healthy faith and healthy wisdom. For Noah's part, he must remember to do what Adam did not; he must remember faith and not eat of one of its trees. Once Noah took care of his own faith, then he could do other things. He could see all the complexities of life and help others discover their own faith. He was his brother's keeper. Well, since his brothers were killed in the flood, he was at least his sons' and grandchildren's keeper too.

Noah knew he needed to support and remember faith at all costs, unlike Adam had done when he harkened to the voice of his wife and went along with her. As we recall, Adam did not handle the situation well, since when Eve handed him the fruit, he simply ate. Adam did not protect his faith. Adam only had to do two things to preserve his faith: tend the garden and not eat from the tree of the knowledge of good and evil. It was as simple as that. But Adam let faith go with little or no thought whatsoever. Now that we know a lot more about faith, we can speculate on what Adam might have done if he were tending his faith instead of going along with Eve.

The first thing Adam should have done to protect his faith was to grab the fruit and throw it as far as he could. Having just undergone thoracic surgery, this may not have been very far, but it would have been a gesture to Eve and the serpent as to where Adam stood. The very next act Adam should have done was to take both Eve and the serpent to the Lord God and see what could be done about the situation. In turn, I imagine that the Lord God would have told them that Eve had to live her life never finding comfort and rest and would suffer shame, fear, worry, sorrow, and desire until she died. Adam, on the other hand, having not eaten the fruit, would have the comforts of faith but would also have to watch his wife suffer and not be able to do a thing about it.

I can't imagine how tormenting that marriage would be. Thinking also about Cain and Abel, what kind of upbringing would they have, with one parent having peace and rest and one parent having no peace or rest? Talk about a split family. It would not have been an ideal situation, but it may have been better than what actually happened. At least one parent would have been capable of passing down the virtues of faith. As it turned out, neither Adam nor Eve could help Cain find faith. Noah had to do a better job than Adam if he was going to be a good keeper of his faith and the faith of his descendants.

Come to think of it, Noah's garden in this part of Genesis 9 is really just a retelling of the garden of Eden story; only this time, I hope that Noah doesn't goof things up like Adam did. Let's look at the next few verses.

> And Ham, the father of Canaan, saw the nakedness of his father, and told his two brethren without. And Shem and Japheth took a garment, and laid it upon both their shoulders, and went backward, and covered the nakedness of their father; and their faces were backward, and they saw not their father's nakedness. (Gen. 9:22–23)

According to Robert Alter,[61] no one has adequately explained the meaning of "Saw the nakedness of his father." Theories range from rape and castration on one hand to disrespect and taboo on the other. None of these ideas seemed to resonate with me. I think the story is begging us to compare the two examples of nakedness that Adam and Eve felt. Noah himself was not ashamed of being naked; he knew he was not perfect, but he had faith to comfort him. Noah experienced nakedness just like Adam and Eve did before they ate from the tree of the knowledge of good and evil. All three were naked and not ashamed. To the contrary, Ham saw his father's nakedness as something to be gossiped about. Ham saw nakedness just as Adam and Eve saw it after they had eaten from the tree of the knowledge of good and evil. Nakedness was something to hide and be ashamed of. Wait a minute—had Ham found the tree of the knowledge of good and evil and taken a bite just as Adam and Eve had? Regardless, Ham was not listening to his faith side.

Of course, all this nakedness is really just a metaphor for being comfortable with whom and what they were. Shem and Japheth knew that they weren't quite ready to see their father's nakedness and not be ashamed, but they did seem to have the wherewithal to cover him up. So to put this unpleasant incident in terms of the rest of the Genesis text, Shem and Japheth were not about to spill any of the faith of their father, like Ham had just done. Next, let's look at how Noah handled the situation and how it compares to how Adam did.

> And Noah awoke from his wine, and knew what his younger son had done unto him. And he said, Cursed be Canaan; a servant of servants shall he be unto his brethren. And he said, Blessed be the LORD God of Shem; and Canaan shall be his servant. God shall enlarge Japheth, and he shall dwell in the tents of Shem; and Canaan shall be his servant. (Gen. 9:24–27)

The story now takes another twist. Instead of addressing Ham directly for what he had done; Noah cursed Canaan, Ham's son. This sounds very misdirected on Noah's part, but it is exactly what God had done to Adam.

61 Alter, Robert. *Genesis: Translation & Commentary*. New York: W.W. Norton and Company, Inc., 1997.

God did not curse Adam directly; He cursed the ground for Adam's sake. God was telling Adam that he himself, without faith, would only produce thorns and thistles. Since Noah did not have the power to curse the ground, he did the next best thing; he cursed Ham's product, his son. Ham's son would only amount to thorns and thistles if Ham rejected faith. Slave of slaves is another metaphor for thorns and thistles.

This was a very clever act on Noah's part. We tend to skip over the intensity of this curse because we don't understand it. But as a parent, I can think of no greater hurt than to think of my parent cursing my child. It brings tears to my eyes even now. Talk about shame, fear, worry, sorrow, and desire all wrapped up into one curse. I think it would hurt so bad that I would have struck out in culpability. "Blame me, Father. Curse me, Father, not my son!" I think this curse may even be a personally stronger one than the one on the ground that God had done. At least I can relate to this personal curse easier than to a global curse of the ground.

Exactly what was Noah so mad about that he felt it necessary to curse his grandson? Well, the way I see it, Noah's number-one job was to support his own faith and the faith of the ones around him. In this story, Noah was symbolically experiencing his faith; he was resting, naked and not ashamed. Although Noah was in his tent, he was demonstrating all the aspects we have come to associate with faith. He was resting like God was on the seventh day of creation, and he was naked and not ashamed, like Adam and Eve were in the garden of Eden. I couldn't ask for a better metaphor. For his part, Ham tried to disgrace Noah's rest or spill his faith. Ham was in serious trouble; he would lose his faith unless Noah stepped in and turned Ham around. It was Ham's faith that Noah was worried about.

Ham was about to lose faith on two accounts. First, Ham had tried to ridicule his father and thereby tried to harm his father's soul, his faith. We all know what happens to people who spill the faith of others; their faith will be spilled. Second, Ham was addressing his father's faults, not his own. Noah knew from his own experience of building an ark that Ham would have to address his own foibles, not his father's. If Ham had any chance at building his own ark, he needed to focus on his mistakes, not his father's faults. If Ham wasn't working on his own ark by now, what chance did Canaan have to build his? So rather than trying to hurt Ham, Noah was being the keeper of everybody's faith; he was looking at the big picture.

Noah also knew from his new covenant with God that God was not going to help Ham to find faith. Noah could not take Ham by the ear to God and ask God to fix him. So Noah did the next best thing he could think of; Noah cursed Canaan. Noah confronted Ham because Ham was using his wisdom to judge his father's nakedness. If Ham chose to see nakedness in terms of shame and something to gossip about, then he, like Adam, would feel all the shame, fear, worry, sorrow, and desire that Adam did. Noah was not going to make the same mistake that Adam did with Eve and Cain. Noah had to take on God's role in the garden of Eden story since he knew God would not curse the ground again. Noah had to do the cursing, not God. It was up to Noah and Noah alone.

Wow, now that's a story! I can now use this story to help me to do the work required for faith. Adam showed me the way not to act, and Noah showed me the way to act. Adam just went along with Eve and lost his faith too. Noah, on the other hand, did not cower and feel embarrassed when Ham tried to dishonor his faith; instead he used the event to try to set Ham straight. Noah told Ham that because he didn't respect faith, his children would suffer the lack of faith too. When someone sheds the blood (faith) of someone else, I hope I will have the courage to follow Noah's example and not be complacent like Adam.

I have to digress here and relate how I initially viewed the story of Noah and Ham. I was very disappointed with Noah in this story; I thought he was supposed to be a hero and all he seemingly did after the flood was get drunk and curse his grandkids. Boy was I wrong, and I am very glad that I see it differently now, especially since I have a son of my own. I now see this story as a retelling of the garden of Eden story, only this time Noah does the appropriate thing and defends faith at all costs and therefore does not have to leave his garden like Adam and Eve had to. Think about it—if Noah felt the shame that Ham had implied, then Noah would have had one foot out of his garden of Eden already. In fact, Noah lived another 350 years in faith, and then he died.

> And Noah lived after the flood three hundred and fifty years. And all the days of Noah were nine hundred and fifty years: and he died. (Gen. 9:28–29)

The next chapter tells us about the descendants of Noah and in particular what happened to Ham's descendants. We might be surprised to find that Ham's offspring did not appear to be slaves; in fact, they were mighty hunters and established great kingdoms. We hear a lot about the accomplishments of Ham's descendants and very little about Noah's two other sons who were blessed and put on the path to great things. What could this be all about?

> Faith is the sense of life, that sense by virtue of which man does not destroy himself, but continues to live on. It is the force whereby we live.
>
> —Leo Tolstoy (1828–1910)[62]

62 ThinkExist.com Quotations. "Leo Nikolaevich Tolstoy quotes". ThinkExist.com Quotations Online 1 Oct. 2012. 20 Nov. 2012 <http://en.thinkexist.com/quotes/leo_nikolaevich_tolstoy/5.html>

That's the thing about faith. If you don't have it you can't understand it. And if you do, no explanation is necessary.
—Kira Nerys (2343–) character on *Star Trek: Deep Space Nine*[63]

Genesis 10

1 Now these are the generations of the sons of Noah, Shem, Ham, and Japheth: and unto them were sons born after the flood

2 The sons of Japheth; Gomer, and Magog, and Madai, and Javan, and Tubal, and Meshech, and Tiras.

3 And the sons of Gomer; Ashkenaz, and Riphath, and Togarmah.

4 And the sons of Javan; Elishah, and Tarshish, Kittim, and Dodanim.

5 By these were the isles of the Gentiles divided in their lands; every one after his tongue, after their families, in their nations.

6 And the sons of Ham; Cush, and Mizraim, and Phut, and Canaan.

7 And the sons of Cush; Seba, and Havilah, and Sabtah, and Raamah, and Sabtechah: and the sons of Raamah; Sheba, and Dedan.

8 And Cush begat Nimrod: he began to be a mighty one in the earth.

9 He was a mighty hunter before the LORD: wherefore it is said, Even as Nimrod the mighty hunter before the LORD.

63 ThinkExist.com Quotations. "Kira Nerys quotes". ThinkExist.com Quotations Online 1 Oct. 2012. 20 Nov. 2012 <http://en.thinkexist.com/quotes/kira_nerys/>

10 And the beginning of his kingdom was Babel, and Erech, and Accad, and Calneh, in the land of Shinar.

11 Out of that land went forth Asshur, and builded Nineveh, and the city Rehoboth, and Calah,

12 And Resen between Nineveh and Calah: the same is a great city.

13 And Mizraim begat Ludim, and Anamim, and Lehabim, and Naphtuhim,

14 And Pathrusim, and Casluhim, (out of whom came Philistim,) and Caphtorim.

15 And Canaan begat Sidon his first born, and Heth,

16 And the Jebusite, and the Amorite, and the Girgasite,

17 And the Hivite, and the Arkite, and the Sinite,

18 And the Arvadite, and the Zemarite, and the Hamathite: and afterward were the families of the Canaanites spread abroad.

19 And the border of the Canaanites was from Sidon, as thou comest to Gerar, unto Gaza; as thou goest, unto Sodom, and Gomorrah, and Admah, and Zeboim, even unto Lasha.

20 These are the sons of Ham, after their families, after their tongues, in their countries, and in their nations.

21 Unto Shem also, the father of all the children of Eber, the brother of Japheth the elder, even to him were children
born.22 The children of Shem; Elam, and Asshur, and Arphaxad, and Lud, and Aram.

23 And the children of Aram; Uz, and Hul, and Gether, and Mash.

24 And Arphaxad begat Salah; and Salah begat Eber.

25 And unto Eber were born two sons: the name of one was Peleg; for in his days was the earth divided; and his brother's name was Joktan.

26 And Joktan begat Almodad, and Sheleph, and Hazarmaveth, and Jerah,

27 And Hadoram, and Uzal, and Diklah,

28 And Obal, and Abimael, and Sheba,

29 And Ophir, and Havilah, and Jobab: all these were the sons of Joktan.

30 And their dwelling was from Mesha, as thou goest unto Sephar a mount of the east.

31 These are the sons of Shem, after their families, after their tongues, in their lands, after their nations.

32 These are the families of the sons of Noah, after their generations, in their nations: and by these were the nations divided in the earth after the flood.

After the Noah story, we find another list of generations. In Genesis 10, each of Noah's sons has a turn at documenting up to four subsequent generations. Even though this chapter tells us that all peoples and all nations are derived from the descendants of Noah, that we all share a common history, the major message of Chapter 10 tells us more about Noah's curse on Ham's family and what faith in action does and does not look like to the outside observer.

To understand the meaning of Noah's lineage, we need to compare it to the ones found in Genesis 4 and 5. We'll first look at the descendants of

Japheth and Shem. Both genealogies merely list the generations. It does not go into any of their accomplishments. Nothing seemed to be happening in their lives. Isn't that funny? Noah had predicted great things for Shem and Japheth, but their descendants are merely listed without any of their worldly accomplishments. This is exactly how the descendants of Seth's were listed in Genesis 5.

I can't help but think that the Bible is telling us that the heirs of Seth, Shem, and Japheth accomplished something much more important than worldly things. Their accomplishments were in the realm of faith, not of material things, and as we already know, things regarding faith can rarely be put into words. Therefore, when working on faith, we remain silent, and from an outside perspective nothing seems to be happening. Take Noah, for example. I think we'll all agree that he rediscovered his faith before he left the ark. If we go back and reread the entire Noah story (don't worry, I'm not going to reprint it here), we will see that he did not say one word while he was building or staying in the ark, not one. Noah did not speak until he spoke in defense of faith. The first words he uttered were to curse Canaan and to inform Ham that if he persisted in turning away from faith, he would only produce thorns and thistles; his children would only be thorns and thistles.

Words of accomplishment do not go with faith. I think we can conclude that Japheth and Shem's offspring had or at least wanted faith in their lives. Ham's lineage, on the other hand, reminds us more of Cain's descendants found in Genesis 4.

Cain's offspring exerted their own will on the world rather than focusing on finding faith. They created music, tools, and trouble. Similarly, and far from being slaves, Ham's children and grandchildren made a name for themselves. For example, Nimrod was a great hunter and made a kingdom for himself. I think the Bible is implying that although Nimrod was great, he was more like Cain than Abel.

Next, we see what happened to Canaan and his descendants. Canaan was far from a slave of slaves, at least in terms of landholdings. His offspring covered a very large territory, and they seemed to be quite in charge of their own lives. But I think again what they had accumulated in physical holdings, they lacked in faith. Their territories included Sodom and Gomorrah. Although we have not gotten to the story of Sodom and Gomorrah, their reputations precede them. This just proves that Noah was right, that Ham's descendants were cursed to be slaves—slaves of their own wisdom, just like the members of the line of Cain.

The take-home message of this chapter is that the real heroes are the descendants of Japheth and Shem. They may not have been great hunters or formed vast kingdoms, but they preserved their reverence for faith. Faith in action not only can be but almost always is silent to the outside world. This silence certainly demonstrates faith in action, and maybe we should listen a little harder for this silence in our own lives. The next chapter will give our final lesson in faith and then link us to the rest of the Genesis story and its main character, Abraham.

> It is not always granted to the sower to live to see the harvest.
> All work that is worth anything is done in faith.
>
> —Albert Schweitzer (1875–1965)[64]

64 ThinkExist.com Quotations. "Albert Schweitzer quotes". ThinkExist.com Quotations Online 1 Oct. 2012. 20 Nov. 2012 <http://en.thinkexist.com/quotes/albert_schweitzer/6.html>

The one who knows himself, knows his Lord.
—Muhammad (c.570–632)[65]

Genesis 11

1 And the whole earth was of one language, and of one speech.

2 And it came to pass, as they journeyed from the east, that they found a plain in the land of Shinar; and they dwelt there.

3 And they said one to another, Go to, let us make brick, and burn them thoroughly. And they had brick for stone, and slime had they for morter.

4 And they said, Go to, let us build us a city and a tower, whose top may reach unto heaven; and let us make us a name, lest we be scattered abroad upon the face of the whole earth.

5 And the LORD came down to see the city and the tower, which the children of men builded.

6 And the LORD said, Behold, the people is one, and they have all one language; and this they begin to do: and now nothing will be restrained from them, which they have imagined to do.

7 Go to, let us go down, and there confound their language, that they may not understand one another's speech.

8 So the LORD scattered them abroad from thence upon the face of all the earth: and they left off to build the city.

65 ThinkExist.com Quotations. "Muhammad quotes". ThinkExist.com Quotations Online 1 Oct. 2012. 20 Nov. 2012 <http://en.thinkexist.com/quotes/muhammad/2.html>

9 Therefore is the name of it called Babel; because the LORD did there confound the language of all the earth: and from thence did the LORD scatter them abroad upon the face of all the earth.

10 These are the generations of Shem: Shem was an hundred years old, and begat Arphaxad two years after the flood:

11 And Shem lived after he begat Arphaxad five hundred years, and begat sons and daughters.

12 And Arphaxad lived five and thirty years, and begat Salah:

13 And Arphaxad lived after he begat Salah four hundred and three years, and begat sons and daughters.

14 And Salah lived thirty years, and begat Eber:

15 And Salah lived after he begat Eber four hundred and three years, and begat sons and daughters.

16 And Eber lived four and thirty years, and begat Peleg:

17 And Eber lived after he begat Peleg four hundred and thirty years, and begat sons and daughters.

18 And Peleg lived thirty years, and begat Reu:

19 And Peleg lived after he begat Reu two hundred and nine years, and begat sons and daughters.

20 And Reu lived two and thirty years, and begat Serug:

21 And Reu lived after he begat Serug two hundred and seven years, and begat sons and daughters.

22 And Serug lived thirty years, and begat Nahor:

23 And Serug lived after he begat Nahor two hundred years, and begat sons and daughters.

24 And Nahor lived nine and twenty years, and begat Terah:

25 And Nahor lived after he begat Terah an hundred and nineteen years, and begat sons and daughters.

26 And Terah lived seventy years, and begat Abram, Nahor, and Haran.

27 Now these are the generations of Terah: Terah begat Abram, Nahor, and Haran; and Haran begat Lot.

28 And Haran died before his father Terah in the land of his nativity, in Ur of the Chaldees.

29 And Abram and Nahor took them wives: the name of Abram's wife was Sarai; and the name of Nahor's wife, Milcah, the daughter of Haran, the father of Milcah, and the father of Iscah.

30 But Sarai was barren; she had no child.

31 And Terah took Abram his son, and Lot the son of Haran his son's son, and Sarai his daughter in law, his son Abram's wife; and they went forth with them from Ur of the Chaldees, to go into the land of Canaan; and they came unto Haran, and dwelt there.

32 And the days of Terah were two hundred and five years: and Terah died in Haran.

UNLIKE THE OTHER CHAPTERS OF Genesis, I'm going to start this one with the end of chapter 11 first. Genesis 11:10–32 links us to the rest of the Bible through the genealogy of Shem. It tells us about Shem's descendants but takes a different branch of Eber's family than we saw in Genesis 10, following his son Peleg instead of Joktan. Peleg's offspring eventually lead us to Abraham and the rest of Genesis. That is very important, but as far as I am concerned, the rest of Genesis—indeed, the rest of the Bible—functions mainly to more fully explain the metaphors that the primeval history has introduced us to. In that respect, the rest of the Bible functions to deepen our understanding of the fundamentals that were presented in the primeval history about faith.

The first nine verses of chapter 11 give us our last lesson of the works of faith; or I might say that it tells us how the works of faith shouldn't be worked. But before we get to that, we must discuss the placement of this story. Genesis 11 does not seem to fit right after the separation of the generations of Noah. They were not one people with one language anymore, as stated in the opening verses of chapter 11. Many scholars suggest that these verses fit best right after Genesis 4 and, as this may very well be the case for a better continuity of the storyline; I don't think we would have understood the message of the chapter if it were positioned there. I, for one, needed to hear Noah's story first as the right way to rediscover faith before I was told how not to do it. I already knew too many wrong ways to look for happiness, peace, and rest on my own. So what, then, is the main message of the first part of Genesis 11?

Genesis 11 tells us about a people who seemed to be frustrated by their own individual attempts to discover faith. They decided that maybe they could find faith in a group effort. After all, weren't they supposed to be their brother's keeper too? Shouldn't they work together and build one tower rather than their own separate arks? So they started to build a tower toward heaven.

In the story, God saw this tower and knew that man would not find faith that way. God knew that man was wasting his time building a tower, if in fact man was looking for faith. Finding faith, once we have lost it, is a personal journey; we have to build our own ark. Our way to back to faith comes when we follow our own mistakes, not other people's mistakes, back to atonement. The right way for me to follow may be in the exact opposite direction of another. We must support each other, but we must help others to build their *own* arks, not the ark *we* think that they need to build. We cannot build a cruise ship to faith.

God, seeing the misunderstanding, went down to them and gave them all their own unique language. They were given their own very personal language with which to discover faith. They were each given their own language so they could build their own arks out of atonements and not waste any more time trying to obtain faith from a collaboratively built tower. Knowing this, it doesn't surprise me that the Bible portrays men of faith as silent, just as the genealogies have pointed out; silence is an indication that those men were at least seeking faith in the right way. Each man's faith is essentially in a different language; no one else would understand it anyway *(except someone trying to do his best at writing a book about faith)*. The people portrayed in the Bible who were silent were the very people building their ark in their own language. Faith does not have an audible language, and the best tool we have for understanding it is the language of metaphor. Remember that Noah was silent through the entire process. Abel, Enoch, Shem, and Japheth never spoke a word; all were examples of faith. On the other hand, Adam, Eve, Cain, Lamech, and Ham all spoke and are good examples of our wisdom, not our faith.

The overall message of Genesis 11 is that we cannot find faith in a group; we cannot collectively build a tower to faith. We must build our own ark to find faith. I believe if I were to have read the Tower of Babel story before the Noah story, I wouldn't have understood the significance of the story. I would have thought that Genesis 11 was simply a story explaining how people developed so many different languages. In other words, I needed to work through the Noah story and come to a greater understanding of faith myself before I could see the tower story as the wrong way to achieve faith. I had to find my faith in my own ark, in my own language. That being said, even if the tower story were placed right after the story of Cain and Abel, it still could make sense. It would still be a story of how not to find faith in a group effort. Can we think of a better group than Cain's family that would have tried to build a tower to heaven, if that's what they wanted to accomplish? Maybe we should read the tower story both before and after the Noah story from now on just to get the full impact of its important message.

This marks the end of the lessons given to us in what is called the primeval history. It is simply the most profound collection of stories I have ever read regarding faith. I will never stop reading them, lest I forget their messages. The stories from the garden of Eden to the Tower of Babel have given us an exhaustive personal discussion on how humans lose their faith and the extraordinary measures it takes to rediscover faith. These stories had all the information about faith that I had been searching for all my life. It confirmed to me that faith was the highest creation of the universe, and I was one of its keepers. I cannot remember a time when I cared more about anything.

> What is this awesome mystery
> that is taking place within me?
> I can find no words to express it;
> my poor hand is unable to capture it
> in describing the praise and the glory that belong
> to the One who is above all praise,
> and who transcends every word ...
> My intellect sees what has happened,
> but it cannot explain it.
> It can see, and wishes to explain,
> but can find no word that will suffice;
> for what it sees is invisible and entirely formless,
> simple, completely uncompounded,
> unbounded in its awesome greatness.
> What I have seen is the totality recapitulated as one,
> received not in essence but by participation.
> Just as if you lit a flame from a flame,
> it is the whole flame you receive.
> —St. Symeon the New Theologian (949–1022)[66]

66 *Hymn.* 1 Koder. SC. Vol. 156. pp. 157-158.

Chapter 6

The Postscript Defining Healthy Wisdom and Faith

Some things have to be believed to be seen.
—Ralph Hodgson (1871–1962)[67]

I HAVE LEARNED THAT FAITH WAS created to comfort me and give me the most profound rest I could ever know. I have also learned that by taking care of my un-cursed garden, both faith and wisdom flourish in my life. My faith comforts me, and my wisdom allows me to see all the complexities of life, all the good and all the evil. This, I feel, is the most ingenious self-perpetuating system I could ever imagine. But I have left out one more function of wisdom. Wisdom is the only mechanism by which we are capable of seeing and marveling at faith. Those of us who choose to see faith will get to see the greatest creation in the universe. Maybe in the end, wisdom was

67 ThinkExist.com Quotations. "Ralph Hodgson quotes". ThinkExist.com Quotations Online 1 Oct. 2012. 20 Nov. 2012 <http://en.thinkexist.com/quotes/ralph_hodgson/>

given to us for that very purpose. I know of a poem that captures wisdom marveling at faith rather well; it's found in Genesis 1–2:4a.

> Overexplanation separates us from astonishment.
>
> —Eugene Ionesco (1909–1994)[68]

68 Eugene Ionesco. BrainyQuote.com, Xplore Inc, 2012. http://www.brainyquote.com/quotes/quotes/e/eugeneione386265.html, accessed November 21, 2012.

17864625R00104

Made in the USA
Middletown, DE
11 February 2015